Scrap Basket
Sewing™

Edited by Vicki Blizzard

HOUSE of
WHITE
BIRCHES
PUBLISHERS
SINCE 1947

Scrap Basket Sewing

Editor: Vicki Blizzard
Managing Editor: Barb Sprunger
Technical Editor: Mary Jo Kurten
Book and Cover Design: Jessi Butler
Copy Editors: Michelle Beck, Nicki Lehman, Mary Martin
Publications Coordinator: Tanya Turner

Photography: Tammy Cromer-Campbell, Kelly Heydinger
Photography Assistant: Linda Quinlan

Production Coordinator: Brenda Gallmeyer
Production Artist: Ronda Bechinski
Production Assistant: Janet Bowers
Technical Artists: Liz Morgan, Mitch Moss, Chad Summers
Traffic Coordinator: Sandra Beres

Publishers: Carl H. Muselman, Arthur K. Muselman
Chief Executive Officer: John Robinson
Marketing Director: David McKee
Book Marketing Manager: Craig Scott
Product Development Director: Vivian Rothe
Publishing Services Manager: Brenda R. Wendling

Printed in the United States of America
First Printing: 2002
Library of Congress Number: 2001089866
ISBN: 1-882138-89-9

Every effort has been made to ensure the accuracy and completeness of the instructions
in this book. However, we cannot be responsible for human error or for the results when using
materials other than those specified in the instructions, or for variations in individual work.

Welcome!

What's the one thing all of us who sew have the most of? Why, fabric scraps, of course. It just seems wrong to discard pieces of perfectly usable fabric left over from clothing or decorating projects, so we end up keeping them, hoping someday to find a use for them!

When planning this book, each of us involved thought about how we could best present projects to you that use up pieces of this and that without having them look like, well ... pieces of this and that. We asked our very best craft sewing designers to do the same, and we think they've done an outstanding job! Our projects are appealing and fresh, and will bring a sense of style, warmth and cheer to your home.

As you turn the pages of this book, think about the scraps you have in your basket (or in boxes on your shelves) and how you can use them to make exciting new projects for your home at very little cost for fabric. And if you're new to sewing and don't have a large collection of scraps? Not to worry, these projects take no more than a yard of fabric, making them very inexpensive to make, even if you have to purchase new fabric to sew them.

Any of the projects in this book will also make great gifts for any occasion—ones you'll be proud to give with love (and no one has to know how little you spent on fabric)!

Be sure to keep this book close at hand—we're sure you'll want to refer to it often!

Warm regards,

Vicki Blizzard

Editor

Contents

The Great Room

8 • Floral Elegance Pillow & Candle Mat

10 • Home Sweet Home Banner

12 • Pet Pals Place Mats

14 • Quilt Block Posies Wreath

17 • Patchwork Charm

The Kitchen

22 • Apple Orchard Kitchen Set

25 • Big Bear Place Mat

28 • Pretty & Pink

30 • Wild West Place Mat & Napkin

32 • Watermelon Denim Apron Set

35 • Nesting Hen Dish Towel

37 • Kitchen Buddies

The Master Bedroom

42 • Americana Starflower Pillowcase Set

44 • Americana Starflower Pillows

47 • Classic Chic Bedroom Set

50 • Floral Tissue Box Cover

52 • Ribbons & Roses Tote Bag

53 • Grandma's Posies Bath Set

56 • Aztec-Style Cosmetic Bag and Glasses Case

The Nursery

60 • Fuzzy Bunny Blanket

62 • Baby Animals Bib Set

65 • Baby Ducky Onesie

66 • Bath Time Fun Hooded Towels

69 • Baby Tote

72 • Berry Special Baby Bib & Burp Pad

76 • Cuddle Buddies Baby Car Seat Cover & Diaper Stacker

The Kids' Room

82 • Denim Duo Dorm Set
84 • Yo-Yo Tic-Tac-Toe Game
85 • Chunky Colors Tote Set
88 • Fresh as a Daisy Door Pillow
89 • Huggy Bears Backpack
92 • Noah's Friends Play Pad &
     Finger Puppets
98 • Silly Critters
101 • Roly-Poly Lamb

The Sewing Room

106 • Sewing Basket
107 • Thread Organizer
109 • Sew Happy Sampler
112 • Heart Pocket Scissors Keeper
114 • Sew Sweet Machine Cover
118 • Sew Sweet Armchair Organizer
120 • "I'm So Cool" Frog Pincushion

The Backyard

126 • Sunflower Bucket
130 • Blue Jeans & Bandannas Picnic Mat
132 • Woven Stripes Rug
133 • Cowgirl Clothespin Corral
137 • Cool Citrus Table Set
140 • Sweetheart Wreath
142 • Folk Art Flag
144 • Autumn Leaves
148 • Embroidered Maple Leaf Pillow

The Christmas Home

152 • Jolly St. Nick Stocking
154 • Christmas Cardinals
160 • Poinsettia Wreath
162 • Christmas Tree Gift Bag
164 • Bluework Snowman
166 • String of Lights Candle Mat
168 • Kris Moose
173 • Sewing Guidelines
176 • Special Thanks

The Private World of Tasha Tudor

Tasha Tudor and Richard Brown

The Great Room

Great ideas abound in this chapter of projects for the most-used room in your home—the family room. Whether you have a separate room for family activities, a fixed-up basement area with a television or consider your living/dining rooms to be multipurpose, these projects will use up scraps from your collection and add a sense of style to your decorating.

Our floral pillow and candle mat set will protect your tabletops from wax drips and add comfort to your couch— all in coordinating colors.

Floral Elegance Pillow & Candle Mat

By Marian Shenk

Put a little fabric and a little lace and trim together to quickly make this pretty decorator duo.

Project Specifications

Skill Level: Beginner

Pillow Size: 18" x 18"

Candle Mat Size: 12½" x 12½"

Materials

- 1 yard floral chintz
- ½ yard burgundy brocade
- 18" x 18" pillow form
- 2½ yards upholstery cord
- ¾ yard burgundy braid cord
- 1 (3½") burgundy tassel
- 1 (1½") button to cover
- 7" lace doily
- 2 yards (½"-wide) decorative braid
- 13" x 13" square of batting
- 4 (½") pink oval stones
- 4 (2") lace medallions
- Fabric glue
- Clear nylon monofilament
- All-purpose threads to match fabrics
- Basic sewing supplies and tools

Instructions

Candle Mat

Step 1. From floral chintz cut a 7" x 7" square. Fold in quarters and place pattern on folded edges as instructed; cut out. Do not add seam allowance.

Step 2. From burgundy brocade cut a square 9¼" x 9¼". Center the floral piece cut in Step 1 and satin-stitch with clear nylon monofilament.

Step 3. From floral chintz cut a 13" x 13" square. Place the square made in Step 2 on-point on the 13" square and satin-stitch with clear nylon monofilament.

Step 4. Pin ½"-wide decorative braid around the scallops and around the burgundy square as shown in the photo. Stitch braid in place with clear nylon monofilament.

Step 5. From floral chintz cut one square 13" x 13". Put mat top and back together, right sides facing, and place on batting square. Stitch around perimeter leaving a 4" opening for turning.

Step 6. Turn mat right side out, press and close opening with hand stitches.

Step 7. Appliqué small lace medallion to each corner of mat. Glue oval stones in center of each medallion as shown in photo.

Pillow

Step 1. From floral chintz cut two squares 18½" x 18½".

Step 2. From burgundy brocade cut one square 13" x 13" and cut in half diagonally. Place triangles together, right sides facing. Place burgundy braid cord along two short sides of triangles between fabric layers and stitch. Turn right side out and press.

Step 3. Center 7" lace doily on triangle and stitch in place with clear nylon monofilament.

Step 4. Cover 1½" button with burgundy brocade and sew to center of doily.

Step 5. Place plain side of triangle on top right side of one floral chintz square for pillow top. Sew to square.

Step 6. Cut and piece 2¼"-wide bias strips from burgundy brocade to make a 2½-yard strip. Center upholstery cord on strip to make corded piping. Pin corded piping around outside of pillow top. Place remaining floral chintz square on pillow top, right sides facing. Stitch around perimeter, leaving a 5" opening for turning.

Step 7. Turn pillow right side out, insert pillow form and close opening with hand stitches. Stitch tassel to point of burgundy triangle. ✄

Floral Elegance Pillow & Candle Mat
Candle Mat Medallion Pattern
Cut 1 floral chintz on folds

Fold

Fold

Home Sweet Home Banner

By Kathleen Hurley

This sweet banner will add color, spirit and warmth
to your great room—the hub of family living and activity.

Project Specifications

Skill Level: Beginner

Banner Size: 14" x 9"

Materials

Note: Colors may be substituted with what is available in your scrap basket.

- 1 piece teal felt 14" x 9"
- 2 strips teal felt 1¼" x 6"
- 1 piece cream felt 11" x 6"
- Scraps of rose, teal, gold, bright blue and leaf green felt
- Scraps of light blue, light green, gold and rose silk ribbon
- Dark brown and gold 6-strand embroidery floss
- Water-soluble marker
- Embroidery needle
- Fabric glue
- 14"–16" dowel rod (or natural twig) for hanging
- Basic sewing supplies and tools

Instructions

Step 1. Enlarge pattern as instructed and trace design elements. Referring to photo for color selection, trace around each pattern piece with water-soluble marker. Cut pieces on traced lines.

Step 2. Carefully immerse pieces in cool water to remove all traces of water-soluble marker. Let pieces air dry; press.

Step 3. Referring to pattern and photo for placement, arrange pieces on cream background and glue in place with fabric glue. Glue cream background piece to teal rectangle. Glue small rose hearts to corners of teal rectangle. Allow glue to dry thoroughly before starting embroidery.

Step 4. With 3 strands of gold embroidery floss, work birds' beaks with satin stitch. Satin-stitch birds' eyes with 3 strands of dark brown embroidery floss. Use outline stitch and 2 strands of dark brown embroidery floss to work bird detail lines.

Step 5. Fold each 1¼" x 6" teal strip in half, bringing short ends together. Place ends behind teal background

**Home Sweet Home Banner
Corner Heart**
Cut 4 rose felt

Home Sweet Home Banner
Enlarge entire pattern 125%

rectangle, 1½" from each outside edge. Pin in place for hanging tabs.

Step 6. With 3 strands of dark brown embroidery floss work running stitch ¼" from edges of cream and teal rectangles, stitching through the hanging tabs to secure them in place. Work running stitch around other pieces as shown on pattern.

Step 7. Wash silk ribbons and iron dry with iron temperature at low setting. Using a 16" length of ribbon in an embroidery needle, work lazy-daisy stitches and French knots as shown on pattern. ✄

Pet Pals Place Mats

By Karin Getz

Since the canine and feline members of our households are really
the ones in charge, aren't they entitled to their own personalized "linens"?

Project Specifications

Skill Level: Beginner

Place Mat Size: 17" x 11"

Materials

Note: Materials are for two place mats

- ½ yard light background fabric
- Bright fabric scraps for appliqué
- 1 color of machine-appliqué thread to contrast with bright fabric scraps
- 1½ yards iron-on flexible vinyl
- 1¼ yard fusible transfer web
- Rotary-cutting tools
- Basic sewing supplies and tools

Instructions

Step 1. Using rotary-cutting tools, cut four rectangles each 17" x 11" from light background fabric and iron-on flexible vinyl. Cut two rectangles 17" x 11" from fusible transfer web.

Step 2. Trace the bone and fish shapes on the paper side of remaining fusible transfer web. Cut out leaving roughly ¼" margin around shapes. Following manufacturer's directions, fuse each to wrong sides of two scrap fabrics. Cut out on traced lines.

Step 3. Fuse small pieces of fusible web to a variety of fabric scraps. Referring to photo, cut in random shapes and arrange on right sides of bone and fish pieces, trimming pieces so they butt and do not overlap and are even with bone and fish outlines; fuse.

Continued on page 16

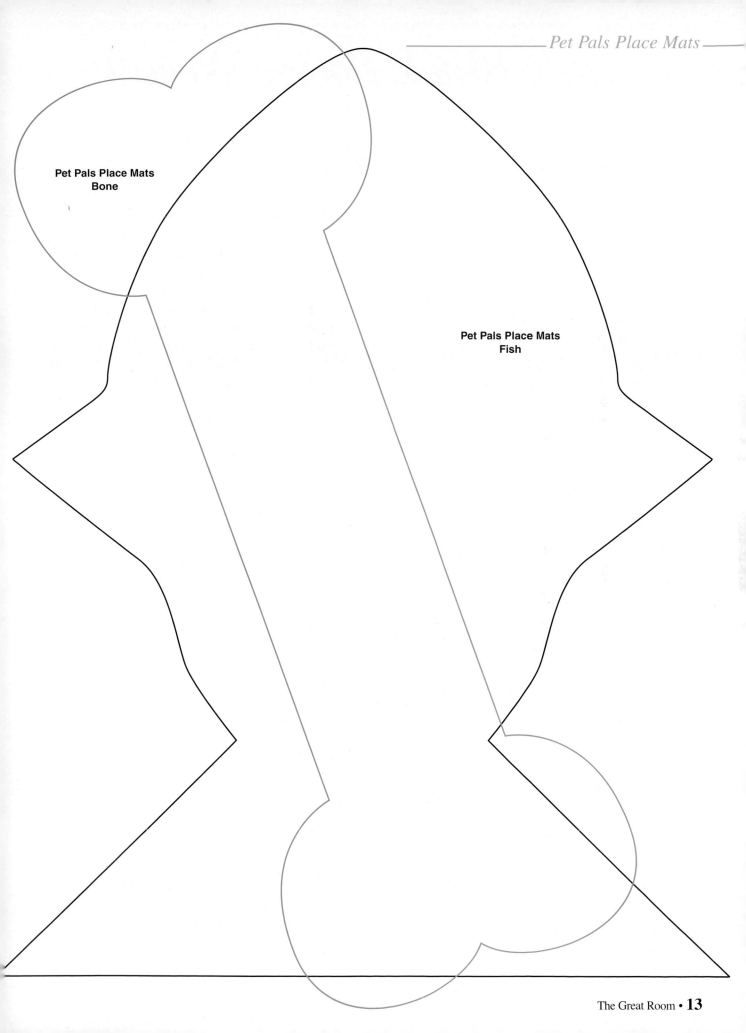

**Pet Pals Place Mats
Bone**

**Pet Pals Place Mats
Fish**

Quilt Block Posies Wreath

By Chris Malone

*Even tiny remaining shreds of a "cutter" quilt can be
fashioned into a lovely memento of a former beauty.*

Project Specifications

Skill Level: Beginner

Wreath Size: Approximately 14" diameter

Materials

Note: Fabric colors can be changed to best match your quilt.

- 14" diameter plastic foam wreath with 2½"-wide flat rim
- 14" x 72", or equivalent, of "cutter" quilt
- ⅛ yard muslin (optional) for backs of flowers
- ¼ yard green reproduction print
- ⅓ yard gold reproduction print
- ¼ yard fleece
- Handful of polyester fiberfill
- 1 spool natural quilting thread
- 1 (¾") plastic ring
- Fabric glue
- Basic sewing supplies and tools

Instructions

Wreath

Step 1. From "cutter" quilt cut or piece two strips 4½" x 72". Sew a wide zigzag stitch along one long edge of each to prevent raveling.

Step 2. Pin one end of strip to back of wreath and spiral-wrap over the wreath, always placing the zigzagged edge on top. When first strip is used, pin end to back and add new strip. When wreath is entirely covered, adjust wraps, if necessary, to make the front of the wreath smooth and even. Remove pins and glue ends in place.

Flowers

Step 1. From the most colorful parts of the quilt cut six large and twelve small petals, one large flower center and two small flower centers. Cut an equal number of petals from less colorful or worn parts of quilt for petal backing. If quilt is very thick, or to conserve quilt, cut backing pieces from muslin.

Step 2. Pin each petal and backing piece together, right

sides facing. Sew a ¼" seam around edges, leaving bottom open. Clip curves and turn right side out.

Step 3. To make each flower, thread needle with double strand of quilting thread. Run gathering stitch along open edge of six petals. Pull thread to gather as tightly as possible. At the end of sixth petal, take a stitch into first petal to form a circle. Make a second row of gathering stitches, pulling circle even closer. Make two small and one large flower.

Step 4. For each flower center, make gathering stitches around edge of circle with doubled quilting thread. Place a ball of polyester fiberfill in center of circle on wrong side. Pull thread up tightly to close. Place centers in appropriate flowers and glue in place over gathered edges of petals.

Leaves

Step 1. On wrong side of green reproduction print, trace seven leaves, leaving ¼" margin between traced lines. Place fabric with traced lines on another piece of green reproduction fabric, right sides together. Place fabric layers on fleece and pin three layers together.

Step 2. Stitch around leaves on traced lines, leaving open at bottom. Cut out ⅛" from seam line and trim tip. Turn right side out. Make a double pleat in each leaf by folding outer edges toward center. Zigzag across bottom edge to finish and hold pleat in place.

Finishing

Step 1. From gold reproduction print cut one strip 8½" x 43". Fold in half lengthwise, right sides together, and draw a 45-degree angle at each short end. Sew long edges together leaving a 3" opening for turning. Sew across angled ends. Trim corners and turn right side out. Close opening with hand stitches; press.

Step 2. Mark center of gold strip with a pin. Fold a 3½" loop each side of center. Gather-stitch through center through all layers and pull thread to shape bow.

Step 3. From gold reproduction print, cut a 3½" x 4" strip. Fold in half lengthwise, right sides together and stitch long edge. Turn right side out and press, placing seam at center back. Wrap over gathered bow center,

overlap ends in back and secure with hand stitches.

Step 4. Referring to photo, arrange bow, flowers and leaves along one side of wreath, using pins to secure. When satisfied with arrangement, lift and glue each piece in place.

Step 5. Sew plastic ring to top back of wreath for hanging. ✂

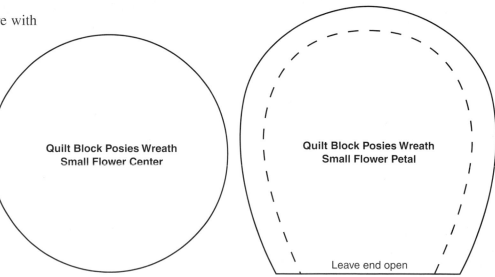

Quilt Block Posies Wreath Small Flower Center

Quilt Block Posies Wreath Small Flower Petal

Leave end open

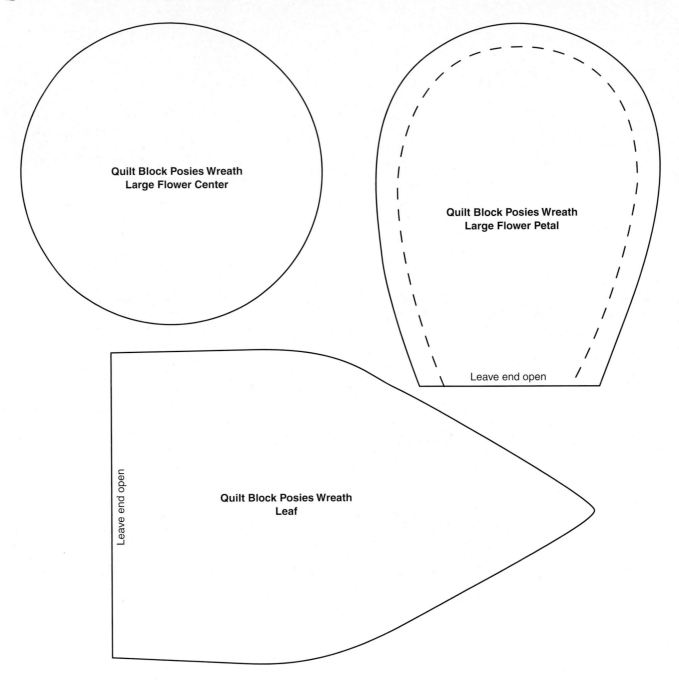

Quilt Block Posies Wreath
Large Flower Center

Quilt Block Posies Wreath
Large Flower Petal

Leave end open

Leave end open

Quilt Block Posies Wreath
Leaf

Pet Pals Place Mats

Continued from page 12

Step 4. Remove paper backing from bone and fish and center each on a fabric background rectangle cut in Step 1; fuse.

Step 5. Fuse one fusible transfer web rectangle cut in Step 1 to the reverse sides of fish and bone fabric rectangles. Remove paper backing. Place wrong side of each remaining 11" x 17" fabric rectangle cut in Step 1 to reverse side of fused bone and fish rectangles; fuse.

Step 6. With contrasting machine-appliqué thread,

zigzag-stitch around fabric scraps and outer pattern outlines of fish and bone. Also zigzag around outer perimeter of each place mat.

Step 7. Carefully following manufacturer's instructions, remove paper from the iron-on flexible vinyl rectangles cut in Step 1. Place sticky side over place mat surface. Fuse as directed. Remember to keep the paper between the iron and the vinyl. Turn the place mat over and repeat on the back. Remove paper from front and back. Repeat for second place mat.

Step 8. Using rotary cutter and acrylic ruler, trim the edges of each place mat, being careful not to cut perimeter edge stitching. ✄

Patchwork Charm

By Pearl Louise Krush

*If you're lucky enough to acquire a quilt beyond repair, use parts
of it to make some or all of the projects in this cozy collection.
If you don't have a "cutter" quilt, purchase an inexpensive new quilt.*

Project Specifications

Skill Level: Beginner

Pillow Size: 14" x 14"

Footstool Size: 8" x 12" x 6" (plus added 14" x
14" pillow)

Lamp Shade Size: 4" x 16" x 9"

Chair Organizer: Approximately 16" x 22"

Materials

For Pillow

- 1 prequilted square 10½" x 10½"
- 1 background square each 10½" x 10½" and
  14½" x 14½"
- 2 rectangles background fabric 10" x 14½"
- 14" x 14" pillow form
- 1 (1½") button

For Footstool

- Wooden footstool 8" x 12" x 6"
- 14" x 14" pillow form
- 1 prequilted square each 14½" x 14½" and
  10½" x 10½"
- 1 background square each 14½" x 14½" and
  10½" x 10½"
- 2 strips background fabric 2" x 44"

- 2 rectangles background fabric 10" x 14½"
- 1 (1½") button
- Paint to match prequilted squares
- Paintbrush
- 1 piece plastic foam 10" x 12" x 1 1/4"

For Lamp Shade

- Self-adhesive lamp shade 4" x 16" x 9"
- 4 prequilted squares 6" x 6"
- ¾ yard background fabric
- 5 (1½") buttons
- Double-wide bias binding to match or contrast
  with fabrics

For Chair Organizer

- 1 prequilted rectangle each 16½" x 22½", 9½" x 16½"
  and 10½" x 16½"
- 2 prequilted squares 6½" x 6½"
- 2 lining pieces 5" x 15"
- 4 yards self-made or purchased binding
- Silica sand, rice or other weighted pellets
- 2 (14") strips hook-and-loop tape or 10 (1") safety pins

For All Projects

- All-purpose thread to match fabrics
- Cool-temperature hot-glue gun and glue
- Basic sewing supplies and tools

Instructions

Pillow

Step 1. Cut prequilted square and 10½" x 10½" background squares in half diagonally. Place a prequilted
triangle and a background triangle together, right sides
facing. Sew the two short sides, turn right side out and
press. Repeat with remaining two triangles.

Step 2. Pin the two triangles, prequilted side up, on
the right side of 14½" x 14½" background square as
shown in Fig. 1.

Step 3. Press under ½" on one 14½" end of each

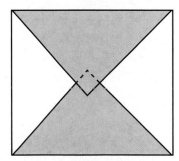

Fig. 1
Pin triangles to background square as shown.

background rectangle. Press under another 1" and
stitch for hem. Align raw 14½" end of each piece with

one pinned end of pillow front, right sides facing. Hems will overlap at the center. Stitch all around perimeter. Turn right side out and sew button to overlapped triangle points at center. Insert pillow form.

Footstool

Step 1. Paint footstool and allow to dry thoroughly.

Step 2. Center plastic foam on wrong side of 14½" prequilted square. Pull the edges of the square firmly to the back of the plastic foam; pin securely. Glue the uncovered side of the plastic foam to the top of the footstool.

Step 3. Make another pillow as shown in Pillow instructions above, but insert pillow form before attaching button. Sew button through all layers of pillow for tufted effect.

Step 4. Fold long edges of each 2" x 44" background fabric strip to wrong-side center of strip; press. Fold each strip in half, aligning folded edges; topstitch.

Step 5. Place the completed pillow on top of the footstool. Slip one strip made in Step 4 through each triangle of pillow. Pull strip ties to underside of footstool and tie securely to finish.

Lamp Shade

Step 1. Peel cover from lamp shade to use for pattern. Place on background fabric, pin in place and cut out.

Step 2. Carefully place background fabric on shade. Fold edge under ¼" and glue in place. Carefully glue double-wide bias binding around top and bottom edges.

Step 3. From background fabric cut four squares 6" x 6". Place each square, right sides together, with a 6" prequilted square. Sew around perimeter leaving one side open for turning. Turn right side out, press and close opening with hand stitches.

Step 4. Referring to photo, arrange prequilted squares around shade, placing buttons between squares. Glue in place to finish.

Chair Organizer

Designer's Note: *This organizer will hold your favorite*

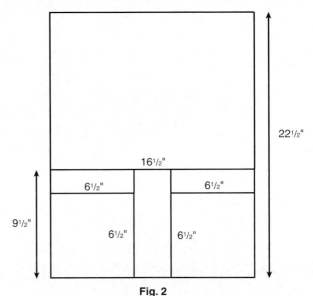

Fig. 2
Arrange pockets on organizer as shown.

magazine, book, glasses, remote control and sewing projects. The weighted pillow makes a great pincushion.

Step 1. Referring to Fig. 2, place the 9½" x 16½" prequilted rectangle on the lower edge of the prequilted 16½" x 22½" background piece for large pocket. Place the two 6½" squares on top for small pockets. Bind the top edge of the large pocket, and the upper and inner edges of the two small pockets.

Step 2. When designated edges of pockets have been bound, pin in place on background. Bind entire perimeter of background piece.

Step 3. Place lining fabric pieces right sides together. Sew two times around three sides, leaving pillow open on one short end. Turn right side out and pour weight product into pillow. Fold the end of the pillow twice and close with hand stitches.

Step 4. Fold the 10½" x 16½" prequilted rectangle in half lengthwise, right sides together. Sew the long edges. Turn right side out and position seam at center back. Bind one end of pillow to close. Insert weighted pillow and bind other end.

Step 5. Sew hook-and-loop strips to pillow and organizer or use safety pins to fasten back of pillow to organizer. ✂

The Kitchen

We all spend lots of time in our kitchens, preparing food, eating meals with the family or just enjoying a freshly brewed cup of coffee with a friend. Decorate your kitchen with some of these cheerful and functional projects that have all been designed in scrap fabrics!

You'll enjoy brightening up your kitchen with the delightful designs we've included in this chapter. (Hint: These projects also make great gifts for a wedding shower or housewarming!)

Apple Orchard Kitchen Set

By Julie Weaver

There are instructions for five projects in this farm-fresh collection.
Search your scrap basket for a variety of tiny red, green and brown scraps.

Project Specifications

Skill Level: Beginner

Bread Cloth Size: 18" x 18"

Place Mat Size: 18" x 12"

Towel Size: 19" x 28"

Pot Holder Size: 9" x 9"

Trivet Size: 10" x 10"

Materials

Note: Natural-color fabric used in models has a woven natural grid, which assists in stitching lines, but any natural-color fabric can be used and grid-marked.

For Bread Cloth

- ⅔ yard green check fabric
- 14½" x 14½" natural-color fabric

For Place Mat

- 2/3 yard green check fabric
- 14½" x 8½" natural-color fabric
- 20" x 14" cotton batting

For Towel

- ⅔ yard green check fabric
- 4" x 20" natural-color fabric

For Pot Holder

- ⅓ yard green check fabric
- 6½" x 6½" natural-color square
- 9½" x 9½" cotton batting

For Trivet

- ⅓ yard green check fabric
- 8½" x 8½" natural-color square
- 10" x 10" square cotton batting
- 12" x 12" square muslin
- 2 muslin squares 11" x 11"
- 6 cups raw rice scented with apple potpourri oil

For All Projects

- Scraps of red, green and brown fabric
- Scraps of fusible transfer web
- All-purpose threads to match fabrics
- Red, green and brown machine-embroidery threads
- Basic sewing supplies and tools

Instructions

Bread Cloth

Step 1. From green check fabric cut two border strips each 2½" x 14½" and 2½" x 18½". Sew shorter strips to two opposite sides of 14½" x 14½" natural-color square; press. Sew longer strips to two remaining sides of square; press.

Step 2. From green check fabric cut a square 18½" x 18½" for lining. Wrong sides together, pin bread cloth to lining. Stitch a 1" on-point grid on natural as shown in Fig. 1.

Step 3. From green check fabric cut 2¼"-wide bias strips and join end to end for an 82" length. Fold lengthwise, wrong sides together; press. Pin raw edges to right side of

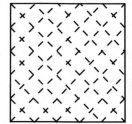

Fig. 1
Stitch a 1" on-point grid
as shown.

bread cloth and stitch. Turn binding to back and hand- or machine-stitch in place.

Step 4. Trace appliqué patterns on paper side of fusible transfer web. Cut out leaving roughly ¼" margin around traced lines. Following manufacturer's instructions fuse to selected fabrics. Cut out on traced lines.

Step 5. Referring to photo, arrange appliqué pieces on corner of bread cloth; fuse.

Step 6. With matching threads and buttonhole or satin stitch, machine-stitch around appliqué pieces. Satin- stitch highlights on apple and veins on leaf.

Place Mat

Step 1. From green check fabric cut a rectangle 14" x 20" for place mat back and two strips each 2½" x 8½" and 2½" x 18½" for borders. Cut two strips on the bias 1¾" x 12"; fold lengthwise, wrong sides together and press.

Step 2. Measure in 1½" from the left side of the 14½" x 8½" natural-color rectangle and draw a vertical line top to bottom. Measure 2½" in from the first line and draw a second line.

Step 3. Position long raw edges of one folded bias strip against first drawn line. Stitch ¼" from raw edge. Press the bias strip over the seam and topstitch in place. Repeat with the second bias strip and the sec- ond drawn line.

Step 4. Right sides together, sew shorter border strips to two opposite sides of place mat; press. Sew longer strips to top and bottom; press.

Step 5. Place batting on wrong side of lining piece. Pin place mat on top of batting/lining. Stitch a 1" on-point

grid on natural as shown in Fig. 1. Do not stitch bias strips and area between. Trim to 18½" x 12½".

Step 6. From green check fabric cut 2¼"-wide bias strips and join end to end for a 70" length. Prepare and bind as in Bread Cloth Step 3.

Step 7. Referring to photo for placement, appliqué apples and leaves as in Bread Cloth Steps 4–6. Note that some pieces are reversed.

Towel

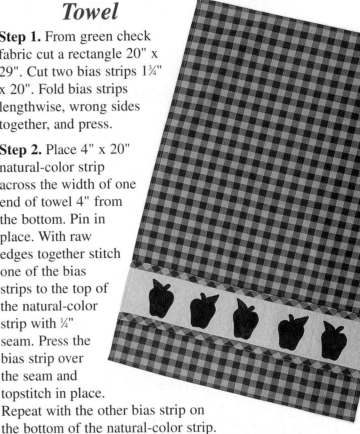

Step 1. From green check fabric cut a rectangle 20" x 29". Cut two bias strips 1¾" x 20". Fold bias strips lengthwise, wrong sides together, and press.

Step 2. Place 4" x 20" natural-color strip across the width of one end of towel 4" from the bottom. Pin in place. With raw edges together stitch one of the bias strips to the top of the natural-color strip with ¼" seam. Press the bias strip over the seam and topstitch in place. Repeat with the other bias strip on the bottom of the natural-color strip.

Step 3. Turn under ¼" on long sides of towel; press. Turn under another ¼" and stitch to hem. Repeat with the bottom and top of towel.

Step 4. Referring to photo for placement, appliqué apples and leaves as in Bread Cloth Steps 4–6. Note that some pattern pieces are reversed.

Pot Holder

Step 1. From green check fabric cut two border strips each 2" x 6½" and 2" x 9½". Cut a square 9½" x 9½" for pot holder back. For hanger cut one bias strip 1½" x 6".

Step 2. Sew shorter border strips to two opposite sides of 6½" natural-color square; press. Sew longer strips to two remaining sides of square; press.

Step 3. Place batting square on wrong side of 9½" backing square. Pin pot holder on top of batting/lining. Stitch a 1" on-point grid on natural-color square as shown in Fig. 1.

Step 4. Fold bias hanger strip in half lengthwise; press. Open and fold raw edges to center fold. Refold strip and topstitch the length of the strip.

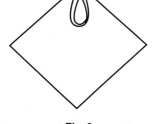

Step 5. From green check fabric cut 2¼"-wide bias strips and join end to end for 46" length. Prepare and bind

Fig. 2
Pin hanger loop to back of pot holder as shown.

as in Bread Cloth Step 3. Before stitching, pin raw edges of hanger to right side of pot holder back as shown in Fig. 2. After binding has been stitched in place turn loop up and tack to binding.

Step 6. Referring to photo for placement, appliqué apple and leaf as in Bread Cloth Steps 4–6.

Trivet

Step 1. From green check fabric cut two border strips each 1½" x 8½" and 1½" x 10½". Sew shorter strips to two opposite sides of natural-color square; press. Sew longer strips to two remaining sides of square; press.

Step 2. Place batting square on 12" muslin square. Pin trivet top on top. Stitch a 1" on-point grid on natural-color square as shown in Fig. 1. Trim to 10½" square.

Step 3. Referring to photo for placement, appliqué apples and leaves as in Bread Cloth Steps 4–6.

Step 4. From green check fabric cut one backing piece each 8" x 10½" and 6" x 10½". Hem one 10½" side on each by pressing under ¼", folding under again and stitching.

Step 5. Place backing pieces, wrong sides together and overlapping, on trivet top as shown in Fig. 3. Pin in place.

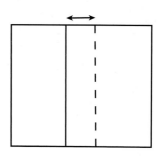
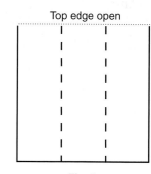

Fig. 3
Overlap backing pieces as shown

Fig. 4
Fold muslin square in thirds as shown.

Step 6. From green check fabric cut 2¼"-wide bias strips and join end to end for a 50" length. Prepare and bind trivet as in Bread Cloth Step 3.

Step 7. Sew 11" muslin squares together on three sides. Turn right side out and press. Turn under ¼" on unsewn edges; press. With unsewn edge at top, fold square into thirds and press as shown in Fig. 4

Step 8. Unfold muslin square and sew on press lines to form three tubes. Fill each tube with 2 cups of scented rice. Close opening with hand or machine

Continued on page 36

Big Bear Place Mat

By June Fiechter

Recycle an old brown wool garment to make this fuzzy-wuzzy friend for a little one in your life.

Project Specifications

Skill Level: Beginner

Place Mat Size: Approximately 15" x 14"

Materials

- 12" x 16" piece of black felt for mat back, nose and eye centers
- Brown wool 12" x 16" for bear face
- 4 pieces brown wool 5" x 6½" for bear ears
- 2 pieces brown wool 6½" x 9" for bear paw
- White fabric scraps for eyes
- 9" x 10" piece of tan print fabric
- 2" x 10" red-and-white pin-dot scrap for collar
- 13" x 15" red-and-white pin-dot scrap for bow (napkin)
- 1½" x 3" red-and-white pin-dot scrap for bow center
- Scraps of thin batting
- Handful of polyester fiberfill
- 1 (½") hook-and-loop circle
- All-purpose brown, black and white thread
- 22" (¾"-wide) tan ribbon for ear trim
- Fabric glue
- Quilt-basting spray
- Fabric-protectant spray
- Powdered cosmetic blush and brush
- Basic sewing supplies and tools

Instructions

Note: Spray fabric back and batting with quilt-basting spray to hold layers together for sewing.

Step 1. Cut pieces as directed on patterns. Trim batting pieces slightly all the way around to fit neatly under fabric pieces.

Step 2. Referring to photo, center tan print fabric and matching batting piece on brown wool bear face. With brown thread zigzag-stitch around perimeter of tan fabric piece.

Step 3. Place wide edge of nose and matching piece of batting at top center of tan fabric piece. With black thread zigzag-stitch around perimeter of nose. With black thread satin-stitch a vertical line from nose to bottom of face.

Step 4. Referring to photo, place white fabric eyes above nose. With black thread stitch around perimeter with satin stitch. Place black felt eye centers and satin-stitch around.

Step 5. Fold 1½" x 3" red-and-white pin-dot bow center lengthwise, both long edges to the center, wrong sides facing; press. Right sides together, glue one short end to bottom center of place mat.

Step 6. Fold 2" x 10" red-and-white pin-dot strip in half lengthwise, right sides together. Stitch across both short ends and turn right side out for collar; press.

Step 7. Center one long edge of collar at lower edge of place mat, right sides together. Stitch to mat, fold down and press.

Step 8. Glue other end of bow center to reverse side of place mat, forming a loop large enough to hold napkin.

Step 9. Right sides facing, sew paw pieces together. Turn right side out; press. Topstitch close to outer edges and along pattern lines to form fingers. Stuff paw area (not arm) loosely with polyester fiberfill. Pin to left side of face near bottom of place mat.

Step 10. Wrong sides together, sew fronts and backs of ears together with batting pieces between. Pin tan ribbon around outer edges of ears and zigzag-stitch in place. Stitch through all layers along straight lines marked on pattern. Referring to photo, pin to top of face.

Step 11. Place face on batting and black felt backing piece. Zigzag-stitch around perimeter of place mat, attaching arm and ears between layers.

Step 12. With black thread, satin-stitch eyebrow lines. With white thread, stitch a highlight on nose and on each eye.

Step 13. Fold arm over to front of place mat to hold silverware. Glue hook-and-loop circles to paw and place mat to hold paw in place.

Step 14. Narrowly hem 13" x 15" red-and-white pin-dot piece for napkin. Fold and pleat and insert into bow center. Fan out into a bow as shown in photo.

Step 15. With brush apply powdered cosmetic blush to cheek areas. Spray place mat with fabric-protectant spray. ✀

**Big Bear Place Mat
Eye Centers**
Cut 2 black felt

**Big Bear Place Mat
Eyes**
Cut 2 white fabric

**Big Bear Place Mat
Muzzle**
Cut 1 tan print & 1 batting
Enlarge 200% before cutting
for full-size pattern

Place on fold

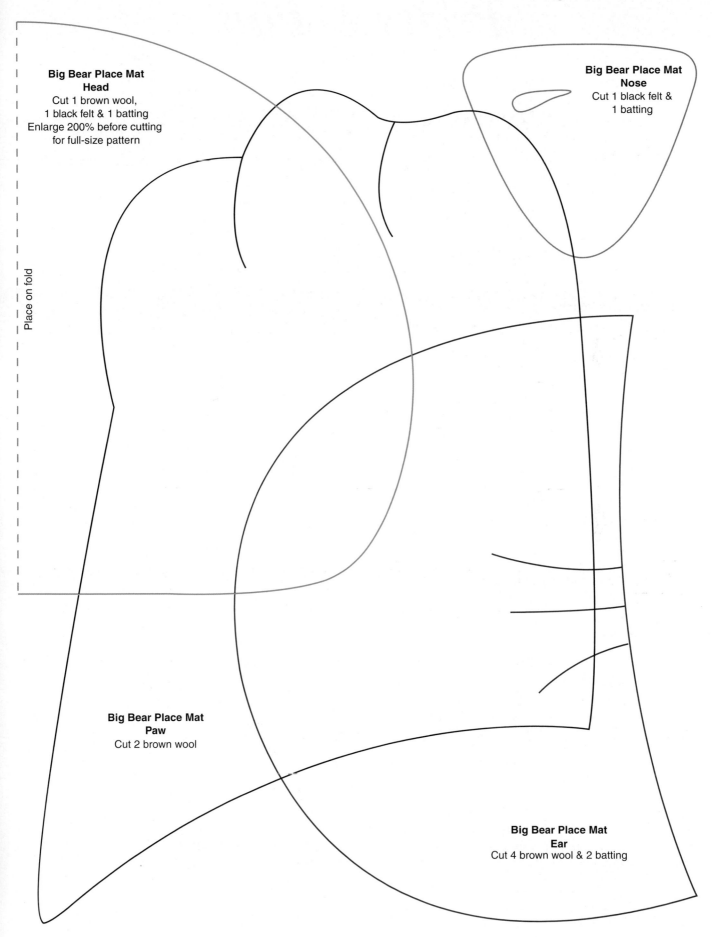

**Big Bear Place Mat
Head**
Cut 1 brown wool,
1 black felt & 1 batting
Enlarge 200% before cutting
for full-size pattern

Place on fold

**Big Bear Place Mat
Nose**
Cut 1 black felt &
1 batting

**Big Bear Place Mat
Paw**
Cut 2 brown wool

**Big Bear Place Mat
Ear**
Cut 4 brown wool & 2 batting

Pretty & Pink

By Pearl Louise Krush

Give your kitchen a face-lift and lift your own spirits
with a soft pastel window treatment and matching chair cushions.

Project Specifications

Skill Level: Beginner

Valance Size: 43" x 9", including tabs

Tier Curtain Panel Size: 21" x 21¼".

Chair Cushion Size: Any size

Materials

For Window Treatment

- 1 pink pastel print fabric strip 10" x 44" for valance
- 2 pink pastel print fabric strips 22" x 24" for tier curtain panels
- 2 pink bias-printed plaid strips 4" x 44" for valance tabs
- 9 (1") flower buttons
- 2 spring rods to fit window

For Chair Cushion

- ⅔ yard pink pastel print fabric for each cushion
- 4 pink bias-printed plaid strips 2½" x 44"
- 4 (1") flower buttons
- Chair cushion to cover

For Both Projects

- All-purpose thread to match fabrics
- Basic sewing supplies and tools

Instructions

Valance

Step 1. Turn under ¼" on all sides of valance strip; press. Turn under ¼" again on two short ends and stitch to hem. Turn under one long edge (bottom) 1" and stitch to hem. Turn under ½" on long top edge; press, but do not hem.

Step 2. Fold each of the two pink bias-printed plaid strips lengthwise, right sides facing, and sew with ¼" seam. From the two tubes cut nine 6" segments. Cut a 45-degree angle at one end of each segment. Sew angle cuts together with ¼" seam. Turn each tab right side out; press, centering seam on back of segment and creating point on front.

Step 3. Place raw edge of each tab under top pressed hem equidistant from each other across top of valance. Pin each tab in place and stitch hem.

Step 4. Bring pointed end of each tab to front of valance, leaving a 1" loop for rod. Sew each tab in place with a flower button.

Tier Curtains

Step 1. Turn under ¼" on all sides of two tier curtain panels; press. Turn under another ¼" on 24" sides of each panel and stitch to hem.

Step 2. Turn under 2" at top of each panel and stitch to hem. Sew another seam ½" from top fold to make rod casing.

Step 3. Turn under another ¼" on lower edge and stitch to hem.

Chair Cushion

Step 1. Fold chair cushion fabric wrong sides together. Place cushion on folded fabric. Cut around cushion allowing 1½"–2" excess around shape.

Step 2. Sew two of the plaid 2½" x 44" strips together end to end for binding. Fold the strip lengthwise, wrong sides together; press.

Step 3. Fold one end of binding in ½". Starting 4" from one end, right sides together, pin and sew binding to top layer of fabric only on the side where cushion will be inserted. Then place both layers of cushion fabric together and sew binding in place around the remainder of the cushion to the open area.

Step 4. Turn folded edge of binding to back of cushion and hand- or machine-sew in place. Insert cushion in open area and hand-sew folded edge of binding to back fabric to close opening.

Step 5. Fold two remaining plaid strips lengthwise, right sides together, for tie strings. Sew with ¼" seam. Turn right side out. Fold ends in and close openings with hand stitches.

Step 6. Pull back corners of cushion cover tight and tie the center of each tie string around gathered corner fabric. Tie a knot.

Step 7. Sew buttons on seat cushion referring to photo to finish. Attach to chair by tying bows in tie strings. ✄

Wild West Place Mat & Napkin

By Bev Shenefield

*Recycle some jeans, add some red bandanna fabric and you'll be
all ready to serve up some mean barbecue on great theme place mats.*

Project Specifications

Skill Level: Beginner

Place Mat Size: Approximately 18½" x 14½"

Napkin Size: 17" x 17"

Materials

Note: Materials are for two place mats and two napkins.

- 1 pair men's denim jeans (single-sewn seam works best)
- 1 yard red bandanna fabric
- 1 yard thin cotton batting
- 4 yards ⅜"-thick sisal rope
- All-purpose red thread
- Buttonhole or quilting thread to match rope
- Basic sewing supplies and tools

Instructions

Note: Instructions are for one place mat and one napkin.

Place Mat

Step 1. Trace and cut place mat as instructed on pattern. Cut eight denim strips 2¾" x 4½". Cut two back pockets from jeans, leaving underlying fabric attached. Trim away excess fabric approximately ¼" from sides and bottom of pocket. Cut underlying fabric ¼" below top pocket edge.

Step 2. Place two cotton batting ovals on wrong side of bandanna oval. Sew around perimeter with ½" seam. Trim batting close to stitching.

Step 3. Stitch top straight edge of underlying pocket fabric with narrow zigzag stitch. Referring to photo, place pocket on denim place mat oval. With red thread

Continued on page 32

Place on fold

Place on fold

Wild West Place Mat & Napkin
Place Mat
For each place mat cut 1 denim,
1 bandanna and 2 batting

Place on leg seams

Watermelon Denim Apron Set

By Connie Matricardi

Summer fun will be further enhanced with these casual, but spirited, kitchen accessories.

Project Specifications

Skill Level: Beginner

Apron Size: Any size

Pot Holder Size: Approximately 8" x 27"

Materials

Note: Cotton batting is recommended for hot pads. Polyester may melt from heat.

- Purchased denim apron
- Denim fabric 8" x 27"
- ⅓ yard red print fabric
- Scraps of black fabric
- Scraps of fusible transfer web
- Cotton batting 8½" x 13"
- 1 package green double-fold bias binding
- All-purpose threads to match fabrics
- Basic sewing supplies and tools

Instructions

Apron

Step 1. Trace and cut watermelon apron pocket as directed on pattern.

Step 2. Trace 19 watermelon seeds on paper side of fusible transfer web. Cut out leaving roughly ¼" margin around traced lines. Following manufacturer's directions, fuse to black scraps. Cut out on traced lines.

Step 3. Turn under ½" along top straight edge of watermelon pocket; press. Turn under another ½" and topstitch to hem.

Step 4. Bind curved edge of pocket with green bias binding. Referring to photo, place on apron front and topstitch on curved edge.

Step 5. Arrange nine watermelon seeds on pocket and fuse.

Pot Holder

Step 1. Trace and cut watermelon hot pad pockets as directed on pattern. Place a pocket at each end of denim strip and cut denim to match curve of pockets.

Step 2. Place two watermelon pieces right sides together. Sew across straight edge with ½" seam. Press seam open. Repeat with other two watermelon pieces.

Step 3. Place one cotton batting piece between fabric layers of each pocket. Trim batting slightly if necessary. Pin one pocket to each end of denim strip. With ¼" seam allowance, stitch around curve to hold in place.

Step 4. Bind perimeter of denim strip, including hot pad pockets, with green bias binding.

Step 5. Referring to photo arrange five watermelon seeds on each pocket and fuse. ✄

Wild West Place Mat & Napkin

Continued from page 30

sew pocket to place mat with zigzag stitch. Sew all edges except top straight edge. As sewn, this will provide separate pockets for napkin and flatware.

Step 4. Fold each 2¾" x 4½" denim strip cut in Step 1 in half lengthwise; press. Bring one long raw edge to center fold; press. Fold other long raw edge under ¼"; press. Bring fold over first long raw edge and topstitch through all layers with red thread. Repeat for eight strips.

Step 5. Fold tabs in half, bringing short ends together, seams on inside. Pin at intervals to right side of denim oval, aligning raw edges, tabs pointed toward center. Stitch each in place, close to edge.

Step 6. Place bandanna and denim ovals right sides together. Stitch around perimeter close to batting and leaving an opening for turning. Turn right side out and close opening with hand stitches.

Step 7. Cut rope in half and thread through denim loops as shown in photo. Tie ends in a square knot at upper left. Secure knot by sewing through rope layers with several strands of buttonhole or quilting thread.

Napkin

Step 1. From red bandanna fabric cut one square 18" x 18". Turn all edges under ¼"; press. Fold all edges under ¼" again and stitch for hem.

Step 2. Fold napkin and place in pocket of place mat. ✄

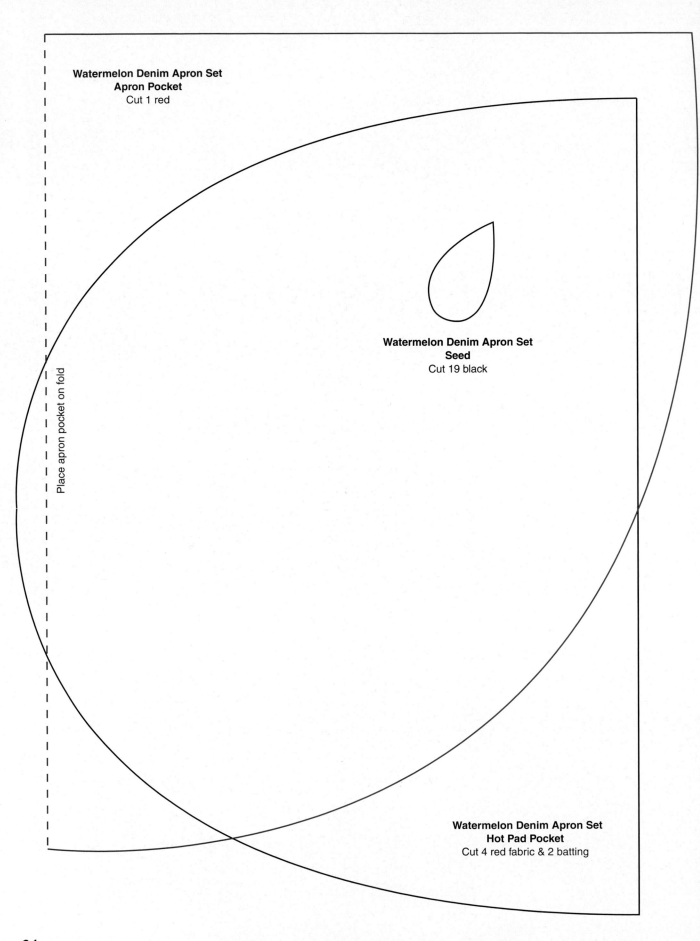

**Watermelon Denim Apron Set
Apron Pocket**
Cut 1 red

Place apron pocket on fold

**Watermelon Denim Apron Set
Seed**
Cut 19 black

**Watermelon Denim Apron Set
Hot Pad Pocket**
Cut 4 red fabric & 2 batting

Nesting Hen Dish Towel

By Mary Ayres

Purchase a neutral dish towel, pull a few little scraps from the scrap basket and faster than you thought possible you'll have this bird in hand to use or to give.

Project Specifications

Skill Level: Beginner

Towel Size: Any size

Materials

- Neutral purchased dish towel
- Scraps of yellow, red, tan, cream and brown
- Black 6-strand embroidery floss
- Scraps of fusible transfer web
- Basic sewing supplies and tools

Instructions

Step 1. Trace pattern pieces on paper side of fusible transfer web. Cut out leaving approximately ¼" margin around traced lines.

Step 2. Following manufacturer's instructions, fuse pattern pieces to selected fabrics, referring to pattern and photo for colors. Cut out on traced lines. Center pieces on towel, 4½" up from lower edge; fuse.

Step 3. Transfer eyes and nostril dots to hen. Using 3 strands of black embroidery floss work buttonhole stitch around all pieces. Make straight stitches for eyes, and wrapping floss around needle one time, make French knots on nostril dots.

Step 4. Measure width of towel. From tan fabric cut a 2" strip that length plus 1". Right sides together, pin strip to lower edge of towel, each end extending ½". Sew ½" from edge. Fold strip to back, folding ends and strip under ½" to form a binding. Sew to backside of towel with hand stitches. ✄

Red

Yellow

Red

Tan

Cream

Brown

Apple Orchard Kitchen Set
Continued from page 24

stitches. Insert through back opening into trivet. Close opening with hand stitches. Remove hand stitches to remove insert for laundering or freshening scent. ✀

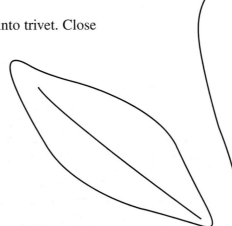

Apple Orchard Kitchen Set Apple Stem
Cut 1 brown for pot holder
Cut 1 brown for bread cloth
Cut 5 brown (reverse 2) at 73% for towel
Cut 4 brown at 73% for trivet
Cut 3 brown (reverse 1) at 63% for place mat

Apple Orchard Kitchen Set Leaf
Cut 1 green for pot holder
Cut 1 green for bread cloth
Cut 5 green (reverse 2) at 73% for towel
Cut 4 green at 73% for trivet
Cut 3 green (reverse 1) at 63% for place mat

Apple Orchard Kitchen Set Apple
Cut 1 red for pot holder
Cut 1 red for bread cloth
Cut 5 red at 73% for towel
Cut 4 red at 73% for trivet
Cut 3 red at 63% for place mat

Kitchen Buddies

By Nancy Billetdeaux

Whimsical, silly little guys strictly for your amusement and distraction when on "kitchen duty."

Project Specifications

Skill Level: Beginner

Buddy Size: Approximately 5" x 4"

Materials

- ¼ yard red print fabric
- ¼ yard green print fabric
- ¼ yard black solid fabric
- 7" x 7" square of black tulle
- ½ yard (⅞"-wide) black-and-white checked ribbon
- ⅜ yard (⅛"-wide) red satin ribbon
- ¼ yard (³⁄₁₆"-wide) black braid
- 7 (12") black chenille stems
- 2 (¼") black barrel pony beads
- 2 (10mm) sew-on moving eyes
- 1 (⅜") white button
- All-purpose threads to match fabrics
- 2 large handfuls of polyester fiberfill
- 7" x 7" square of fleece
- 7" x 7" square of freezer paper
- Compass
- Wire cutters
- Basic sewing supplies and tools

Instructions

Strawberry

Step 1. From red print fabric cut two squares 8½" x 8½". With right sides together, sew around perimeter leaving small opening for turning. Turn right side out, press and close opening with hand stitches.

Step 2. Fold square in half; press. Bring right corner up until side edge is even with top edge; press. Repeat with left corner as shown in Fig. 1.

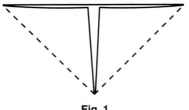

Fig. 1
Fold square in half. Bring each corner up to center as shown.

Step 3. From green print fabric cut four pieces each 1½" x 12" and 1½" x 6". Right sides together, stitch along long raw edges of each piece and

across one short end. Turn right side out and press for two arms and two legs.

Step 4. Place a small amount of fiberfill at the short closed end of each piece and then tie a knot above it. Turn upper raw edges of each piece ¼" to inside and close opening with hand stitches.

Step 5. Unfold right and left corners of red print fabric square and pin unknotted end of legs to upper edge of body as shown n Fig. 2. Bring corners back to center and stitch legs through first layer of fabric square.

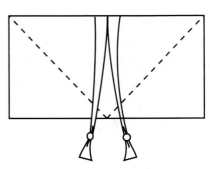

Fig. 2
Open folds and pin legs to upper body edge.

Step 6. Make another fold each side of red print body piece and pin an arm within each fold as shown in Fig. 3. Stitch folds and arms to first layer of body square along upper edge. Stuff the pocket formed with polyester fiberfill.

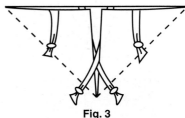

Fig. 3
Fold upper corners again to enclose arms as shown.

Step 7. Use compass to draw a 6½" circle on red print fabric. Turn under ¼" to inside and run a basting thread all around. Pull up tightly to form a yo-yo head that fits body. Tie a knot to secure and stuff lightly with polyester fiberfill. Flatten and whipstitch to body.

Step 8. Referring to photo for placement, sew moving eyes to head. Tie ⅛"-wide red satin ribbon around neck.

Step 9. Trace berry stem on freezer-paper square and cut out. From green print fabric cut two squares 7" x 7". Press freezer-paper stem to right side of one green print square. Place second green print square right side down on work surface. Top with 7" fleece square and place square with freezer paper on top, right side up. Pin layers together. Sew all around stem; trim close to

stitches. Remove freezer paper and sew white button to center of stem.

Step 10. With hand stitches tack stem to strawberry head and knot to secure.

Ladybug

Step 1. Prepare ladybug body as in Strawberry Steps 1 and 2. Stitch folded corners to first layer of body fabric only.

Step 2. Make another fold each side of body bringing points to the back as shown in Fig. 4. Stitch top edges to top layer of body only. Stuff the pocket formed with polyester fiberfill.

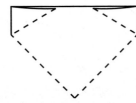

Fig. 4
Bring corner folds to back of body
as shown.

Step 3. Use compass to draw a 5¾" circle on black solid fabric. Place black tulle on right side of circle and pin in place. Cut black fabric and black tulle together. With fabric layers together, complete head as in Strawberry Step 7. Before stitching head to body take a few stitches at center front of head. Lay thread across head to center back. Pull thread snug and take a few stitches to back of head to secure.

Step 4. Stitch head to body. Attach black braid around head with small hand stitches.

Step 5. Cut an 8" length from one chenille stem. Fold in half and attach fold at center back of head, taking several stitches to secure. Thread a black barrel pony bead to each end of chenille stem, twisting to secure bead.

Step 6. Tie ⅞"-wide black-and-white checked ribbon in a bow and tack to base of back of head.

Step 7. From solid black fabric cut four strips 1½" x 9" for back legs and two strips 1½" x 7" for front legs. Fold each leg piece in half lengthwise, wrong sides together; press. Unfold each piece and bring each long edge to meet center fold; press. Fold in half again, bringing folded edges together; press. Fold each short edge in ½". Stitch close to long edge of each leg.

Step 8. Insert a chenille stem in each leg and with wire cutters trim excess length. Stitch short ends close to edge.

Step 9. Tie two knots in each leg and stitch to body, referring to photo for placement. ✄

**Kitchen Buddies
Strawberry Stem**

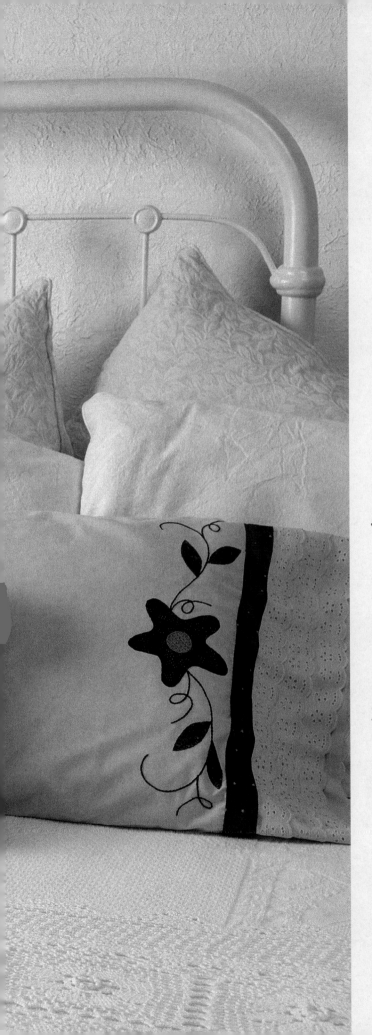

The Master Bedroom

Studies show that our bedrooms have become much more than a place for sleeping at the end of the day. They've become our safe havens—places of retreat for escape from everyday cares and worries.

The projects featured in this chapter will help make your bedroom suite a cozy, comfortable place in which to spend time reading a book, having a private conversation away from the rest of the family or just daydreaming!

Americana Starflower Pillowcase Set

By Julie Weaver

*Trim purchased, plain cases and pair them with the
Americana Starflower Pillows for a grand old look!*

Project Specifications

Skill Level: Beginner

Pillowcase Size: Queen size (easily adjustable for
any size)

Materials

Note: Materials are for two pillowcases.

- 1 pair ecru queen-size pillowcases
- 7½ yards 4"-wide flat ecru eyelet lace trim
- ¼ yard red print for border and binding
- Scraps of fusible transfer web
- Navy, green and gold scraps for appliqué
- Navy, green and gold 6-strand embroidery floss
  to match appliqué scraps
- Water-soluble marker
- All-purpose threads to match fabrics
- Basic sewing supplies and tools

Instructions

Step 1. Measure around pillowcase and add 2". Cut
three lengths of 4"-wide flat ecru eyelet lace trim that
length. Hem each short end with ¼" hem. If top edge
of lace is unhemmed, turn under at least ¼" and press.

Step 2. Starting at center back of pillowcase, pin first
layer of lace so that bottom edge is slightly longer
than hem of pillowcase. Overlap at center back. Stitch
in place.

Step 3. Again, starting at center back, pin second layer
of lace overlapping first layer. Exact placement will
vary depending on style of lace. Repeat for third layer
of lace.

Step 4. Using measurement obtained in Step 1, cut
one 2½"-wide border strip that length from red print.
Hem each short end with ¼" hem. Fold strip in half
lengthwise, wrong sides together; press.

Step 5. Starting at center back of pillowcase, pin border

strip over top layer of lace, aligning raw edges with top edge of lace. Stitch in place, overlapping at center back.

Step 6. Using measurement obtained in Step 1, cut one 1½"-wide binding strip that length from red print. Hem each short end with ¼" hem. Fold binding strip in half lengthwise, wrong sides together; press.

Step 7. Starting at center back of pillowcase, pin binding strip over border strip, aligning all raw edges. Stitch in place, overlapping at center back. Press strip up toward pillowcase and topstitch in place.

Step 8. Trace appliqué shapes on paper side of fusible transfer web as directed on patterns. Cut out leaving approximately ¼" margin around traced lines. Following manufacturer's instructions, fuse to selected fabrics. Referring to photo, position starflower on pillowcase and fuse.

Step 9. With 3 strands of matching embroidery floss, work buttonhole stitch around flower and flower center.

Step 10. Trace vines on pillowcase with water-soluble marker. Chain-stitch traced lines with 3 strands of green embroidery floss.

Step 11. Referring to photo, arrange leaves along vine; fuse. With 3 strands of green embroidery floss, chain-stitch veins on leaves and work buttonhole stitch around edges.

Step 12. Repeat steps above for second pillowcase. ✂

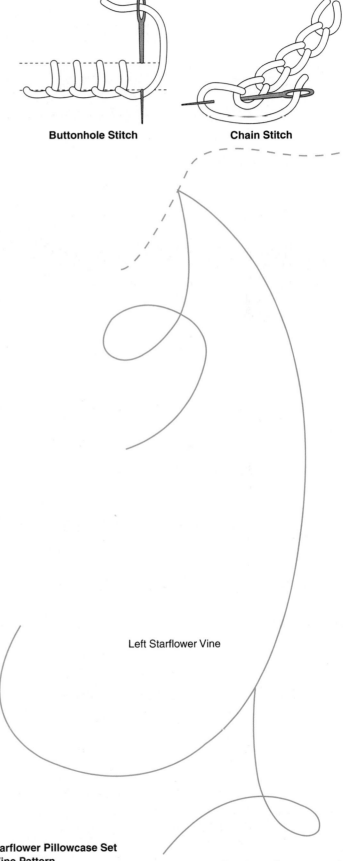

Buttonhole Stitch   **Chain Stitch**

Right Starflower Vine

Left Starflower Vine

**Americana Starflower Pillowcase Set
Vine Pattern**

Continued on page 46

Americana Starflower Pillows

By Julie Weaver

Step up with red, white and blue to lend color and a patriotic statement to your decor.

Project Specifications

Skill Level: Beginner

Pillow Sizes: 12" x 12" and 14" x 14"

Materials

For 12" Pillow

- ½ yard cream print
- ⅛ yard red print
- ⅔ yard navy print
- 13" x 13" muslin
- 12" pillow form

For 14" Pillow

- ¼ yard cream print
- ¼ yard red print
- ⅞ yard navy print
- 15" x 15" muslin
- 14" pillow form

For Both Pillows

- Scraps of navy, gold and green for appliqué
- Navy, gold and green 6-strand embroidery floss to match appliqué scraps
- Scraps of fusible transfer web
- Water-soluble marker
- All-purpose threads to match fabrics
- Basic sewing supplies and tools

Instructions

Note: Use ½" seams throughout and press seams open.

12" Pillow

Step 1. Fold 13" x 13" muslin square in half diagonally. From cream print cut a triangle the same size as the folded muslin triangle, adding ½" to the long diagonal side for seam allowance.

Step 2. From cream print fabric cut one strip 3" x 12", two strips 3" x 8" and 2 strips 3" x 4". From red print cut two strips each 3" x 10" and 3" x 6". Arrange pieces as shown in Fig. 1 and sew.

Step 3. Using the folded muslin triangle as a pattern, cut a triangle from the strips sewn in Step 2, adding ½"

to the long diagonal side for seam allowance.

Step 4. Sew the striped triangle and the cream print triangle together on the long diagonal side.

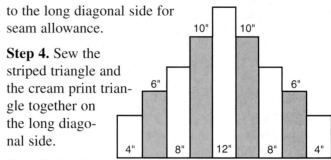

Fig.1
Arrange and stitch strips as shown.

Step 5. Pin the pillow top on the muslin square. To hold layers together, topstitch on cream print ¼" from edge of stripes and large triangle.

Step 6. Trace appliqué shapes on paper side of fusible transfer web as directed on patterns. Cut out leaving approximately ¼" margin around traced lines. Following manufacturer's instructions, fuse to selected fabrics. Referring to photo, position on cream triangle and fuse.

Step 7. With 3 strands of matching embroidery floss, work buttonhole stitch around appliqués. Chain-stitch veins on leaves.

Step 8. Referring to photo, use water-soluble marker to draw vining tendrils around leaves and flowers. Chain-stitch traced lines with 3 strands of green embroidery floss.

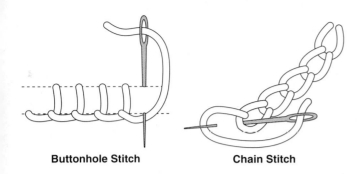

Buttonhole Stitch   **Chain Stitch**

Step 9. Cut two 5" strips across width of navy print. Join short ends to make a circle. Fold circle in half, bringing raw edges together; press. Divide circle in four equal parts and mark with pins. Sew four sets of gathering stitches that begin and end at each segment. Pull up gathers and sew a gathered segment to each edge of pillow top, aligning raw edges.

Step 10. From navy print cut two pieces 9" x 13". Hem one 13" side of each piece. With right sides together, pin backing pieces to pillow top, overlapping hemmed backing edges at center. Stitch around perimeter.

Step 11. Turn right side out and insert pillow form to finish.

14" Pillow

Step 1. From cream print fabric cut three strips 3" x 15". From red print fabric cut four strips 3" x 15". Arrange pieces as shown in Fig. 2 and sew.

Step 2. Place striped piece on 15" muslin square. To hold layers together, topstitch ¼" from edge of each stripe with matching threads.

Step 3. Trace appliqué shapes on paper side of fusible transfer web as directed on patterns. Cut out leaving approximately ¼" margin around traced lines. Following manufacturer's instructions, fuse to selected fabrics. Referring to photo, position on pillow top and fuse.

Step 4. With 3 strands of matching embroidery floss, work buttonhole stitch around appliqués. Chain-stitch veins on leaves.

Step 5. Referring to photo, use water-soluble marker to draw vining tendrils around leaves and flowers. Chain-stitch traced lines with 3 strands of green embroidery floss.

Step 6. Cut three 5" strips across width of navy print. Make and sew ruffle as in Step 9 above.

Step 7. From navy print cut two pieces 10" x 15". Finish pillow as in Steps 10 and 11 above. ✄

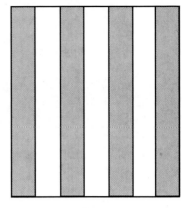

Fig. 2
Arrange and stitch strips as shown.

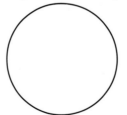

Americana Starflower Pillows
12" Pillow
Starflower Center
Cut 1 gold

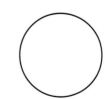

Americana Starflower Pillows
14" Pillow
Starflower Center
Cut 3 gold

Americana Starflower Pillows
14" Pillow
Leaf
Cut 4 green

Americana Starflower Pillows
12" Pillow
Leaf
Cut 3 green

Americana Starflower Pillows
12" Pillow
Starflower
Cut 1 navy

Americana Starflower Pillows
14" Pillow
Starflower
Cut 3 navy

Americana Starflower Pillowcase Set

Continued from page 43

Americana Starflower Pillowcase Set
Starflower
Cut 2 navy

Americana Starflower Pillowcase Set
Starflower Center
Cut 2 gold

Americana Starflower Pillowcase Set
Leaf
Cut 8 green

Classic Chic Bedroom Set

By Pearl Louise Krush

Combine velvets and a rich floral print to make these beautiful,
yet absolutely functional, items for a pretty bedroom.

Project Specifications

Skill Level: Beginner

Jewelry Roll Size: Approximately 8½" x 11" (open)

Heart Sachet: Approximately 4" x 5"

Basket: Approximately 8½" x 11"

Materials

- 1 yard floral print fabric
- ⅛ yard green velvet
- ¼ yard burgundy velvet
- ¼ yard thin cotton batting
- Small amount of polyester fiberfill
- Small amount of potpourri
- 5 (¾") buttons
- 8½" x 11" purchased basket
- Cardboard to fit inside bottom of basket
- Cool-temperature glue gun and glue
- All-purpose threads to match fabrics
- Basic sewing supplies and tools

Instructions

Basket

Step 1. Use cardboard as a pattern to cut batting the same size. Place cardboard on floral print fabric and cut fabric ½" larger than cardboard all around.

Step 2. Place floral fabric piece right side down on work surface. Center batting and then cardboard on top. Place a small spot of glue at each corner of cardboard. Pull corners of fabric onto glue. Glue all edges of fabric to cardboard.

Step 3. From floral print cut two 6" strips across the width of the fabric. Sew together end to end. Fold lengthwise, wrong sides together; press.

Step 4. Fold one end of strip 1" to inside. Starting 2" from folded end of floral fabric strip, finger-press 1½" pleats along raw edges the full length of the strip. Stitch pleats in place.

Step 5. Spot-glue raw edges of pleated strip to bottom edge of basket. Overlap ends. Trim excess fabric,

leaving about 1". Slip end into folded end of pleated ruffle. Glue in place.

Step 6. Measure around perimeter of covered cardboard. Cut a 1½" strip of burgundy velvet that length plus 1½". Fold in half lengthwise, wrong sides together. Fold one short end under ¾". Glue raw edges of velvet strip over raw edges of floral strip at bottom edge of basket. Slip end into folded end of strip.

Step 7. From burgundy velvet cut two strips 1½" x 10". Place strips right sides together and sew along both long edges. Turn right side out. Referring to photo, place ribbon diagonally across covered cardboard made in Step 2. Pull ends to backside and glue.

Step 8. Glue covered cardboard to inside bottom of basket. Glue three buttons on diagonal velvet strip, referring to photo for placement.

Heart Sachet

Step 1. From floral print fabric cut three strips 1½" x 8". From burgundy and green velvet cut one strip each 1½" x 8". Sew strips together alternating velvet strips between floral strips.

Step 2. Place heart pattern diagonally on stripped fabric panel as shown in Fig. 1. Trace and cut out. Cut another heart from burgundy velvet.

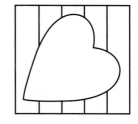

Fig. 1
Place heart pattern diagonally on stripped panel as shown.

Step 3. Place hearts right sides together and sew around perimeter leaving 2" opening on one side. Turn right side out and stuff with polyester fiberfill and potpourri. Close opening with hand stitches.

Step 4. From burgundy velvet cut one strip 1½" x 10". Fold in half lengthwise and stitch long edge. Turn right side out. Turn ends to inside and stitch. Stitch two ends together at top of heart for hanger. Glue or sew button in place as shown in photo.

Jewelry Roll

Step 1. From floral print cut two pieces 8½" x 11". From batting and burgundy velvet cut one piece each 8½" x 11".

Step 2. Place burgundy velvet piece right side down on work surface. Place batting on top and one floral print piece right side up on top of batting. Fold remaining floral fabric piece in half, bringing wrong sides of short ends together. Place on top of layered piece, aligning raw edges at bottom.

Step 3. From burgundy velvet cut one piece 6" x 8½". Fold in half, bringing wrong sides of 8½" ends together. Place on top of layered pieces, aligning raw edges at bottom as shown in Fig. 2. Sew a ¼" seam around perimeter to hold layers together.

Step 4. From green velvet cut one 2½" strip across the width of the fabric. Fold strip lengthwise, wrong sides together. Sew raw edges of strip around perimeter of jewelry roll, overlapping ends. Bring folded edge of strip to the back and hand-stitch in place.

Step 5. From green velvet cut one strip 2½" x 5". Fold in half lengthwise, right sides together. Turn right side out. Turn ends to inside and stitch. Overlap ends and stitch to inside of jewelry roll to form loop for button.

Step 6. Roll case and sew button in appropriate place to fasten with loop. ✄

Print

Fold

Print

Fold

Velvet

Fig. 2
Layer fabric pockets as shown.

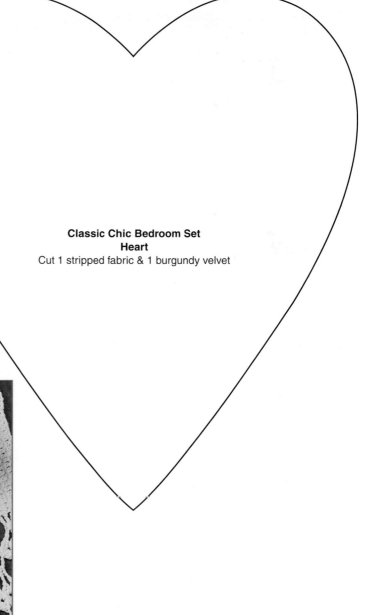

Classic Chic Bedroom Set
Heart
Cut 1 stripped fabric & 1 burgundy velvet

Floral Tissue Box Cover

By Joanne S. Bembry

Retrieve a few fabric scraps from decorating your master bedroom and fashion a reversible tissue cover that will blend with the decor.

Project Specifications

Skill Level: Beginner

Tissue Box Cover Size: Approximately 4½" x 5½" x 4½"

Materials

- 13" x 18" floral print fabric for outer tissue box cover
- 13" x 18" coordinating floral print fabric for tissue box cover lining
- Scraps of coordinating fabrics for appliqué
- 48" (¼"-wide) coordinating satin ribbon
- Scraps of fusible transfer web
- 4" x 6" piece of fusible interfacing
- Water-soluble marker
- All-purpose threads to match fabrics
- Basic sewing supplies and tools

Instructions

Step 1. Trace appliqué shapes on paper side of fusible transfer web as directed on patterns. Cut out leaving roughly ¼" margin around shapes. Following manufacturer's instructions, fuse to selected fabric scraps; cut out on traced lines.

Step 2. Center fusible interfacing on wrong side of outer tissue box fabric as shown in Fig. 1. Fuse as directed in manufacturer's instructions.

Step 3. On right side of fused fabric find center and mark with water-soluble marker. Measure 4" up from bottom edge and draw two stems as shown in Fig. 2. Use a narrow zigzag or satin stitch to cover stem.

Step 4. Referring to photo, position flowers and leaf appliqué pieces; fuse. Finish all appliqué edges with satin stitch.

Step 5. Fold appliquéd fabric piece in half, right sides facing, bringing short ends together. Stitch with ¼" seam; press seam open.

Step 6. Place fabric flat with seam centered as shown in Fig. 3. Stitch across bottom to join layers.

Step 7. Repeat Steps 5 and 6 with tissue box cover lining fabric.

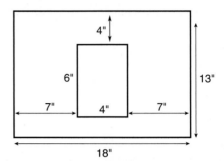

Fig. 1
Center fusible interfacing on wrong side of fabric as shown.

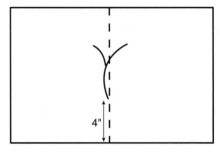

Fig. 2
Mark stems on fabric as shown.

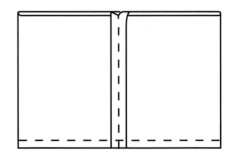

Fig. 3
Place fabric with seam centered as shown. Stitch across bottom.

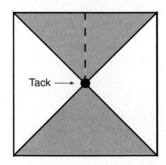

Fig. 4
Tack outside corners together as shown.

Step 8. Slip one cover inside the other, right sides facing and seams aligned. Pin raw edges together. Stitch around top edge leaving 2½" opening. Turn right side out through opening; press. Close opening with hand stitches.

Step 9. Pull outside corners toward center. Tack points together to join to outer layer to form bottom of cover as shown in Fig. 4. Repeat for lining.

Step 10. Cut two 24" lengths of ¼"-wide satin ribbon. Fold one piece in half and tack center point to outer fabric seam line 2" from top edge. Repeat with second piece of ribbon, tacking to seam of lining.

Step 11. Insert tissue box in cover. Gather fabric edges together and tie with loose bow in front. Pull

tissue up through center of gathers. For a change in decor, turn the cover inside out. ✄

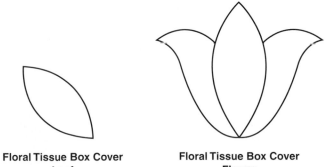

**Floral Tissue Box Cover
Leaf
Cut 2**

**Floral Tissue Box Cover
Flower
Cut 2**

Ribbons & Roses Tote Bag

By Marian Shenk

*Make this bag with fabrics that coordinate with your bedroom decor,
then keep it near at hand for stashing and toting.*

Project Specifications

Skill Level: Beginner

Tote Bag Size: Approximately 11½" x 14" x 2"

Materials

- ½ yard natural canvas
- ½ yard burgundy print for lining
- Scraps of pink, green and burgundy prints
- 2 packages wide burgundy bias tape
- 14 small ribbon roses in shades of pink
- All-purpose threads to match fabrics
- Hot-glue gun and glue
- Basic sewing supplies and tools

Instructions

Step 1. From natural canvas and burgundy print cut two pieces each 11½" x 14"

Step 2. From assorted print scraps cut 64 squares 2" x 2". Sew squares together as shown in Fig. 1 to make two hearts; press.

Step 3. Position and baste hearts to each piece of canvas as shown in Fig. 2. Trim canvas at top edges to

Continued on page 57

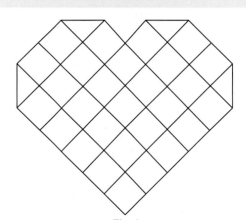

Fig. 1
Sew squares together as shown
to make 2 hearts.

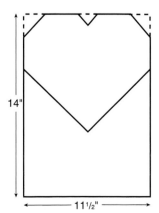

14"

11¹/₂"

Fig. 2
Position and baste hearts to canvas
front and back.

Grandma's Posies Bath Set

By Pearl Louise Krush

Chenille is back, reproduction fabrics abound and everyone loves yo-yos. Put them all together to make a fashionably nostalgic collection for your bathroom.

Project Specifications

Skill Level: Beginner

Size: Each piece, any size

Materials

- Purchased chenille bathroom rug
- ⅔ yard chenille to match purchased rug (yardage may need to be adjusted if required by your pattern)
- ½ yard reproduction print for large yo-yos
- ⅛ yard reproduction print for small yo-yos
- ¼ yard green reproduction print for leaves and stems
- 2½ yards (¼"-wide) elastic
- 1 (1") safety pin
- All-purpose threads to match fabrics
- Pattern paper
- Basic sewing supplies and tools

Instructions

Embellishment

Step 1. Cut yo-yo circles from reproduction prints as directed on patterns. Turn outer edge of yo-yo circles ¼" to inside. Double-thread needle and knot. Make gathering stitches around outer edge. Pull gathering stitches tight and tie off. Repeat for nine large yo-yos and nine small yo-yos.

Step 2. Cut leaf shapes as directed on pattern. Place two pieces right sides together and sew completely around perimeter using a ¼" seam allowance. Carefully cut a 2" slit in one layer of fabric and turn right side out; press. Repeat for six leaves.

Step 3. From green reproduction fabric cut three strips 1¼" x 8" and six strips 1¼" x 4½". Fold each strip lengthwise, wrong sides together for stems; press. Put yo-yos, leaves and stems aside.

Lid Cover

Step 1. Slip pattern paper under toilet lid and trace around perimeter. Add 3" all around shape. Determine desired direction of chenille rows, pin pattern in place and cut fabric.

Step 2. Referring to photo, arrange yo-yos, leaves and stems on fabric. Sew ¼" seam along raw edges of stems. Bring folded edges and ends of stems over seams and stitch in place by hand or machine. Stitch yo-yo flowers and leaves in place by hand or machine.

Step 3. Turn under edge of chenille ½" and then again 1" for hem. Sew around perimeter leaving 1" open. Insert safety pin in end of ¼"-wide elastic and thread through hem channel. Place cover on lid and pull elastic until cover fits lid snugly. Knot ends of elastic together and allow to slip into the hem.

Tank Topper

Step 1. Make paper pattern same as for Lid Cover. Repeat Lid Cover Steps 1–3. Adjust elastic to fit tank top.

Rug

Step 1. Attach yo-yo flowers, leaves and stems as above, but place a piece of paper over the rubber backing on the reverse side of the rug. This will make it easier to move the rug through the machine. ✂

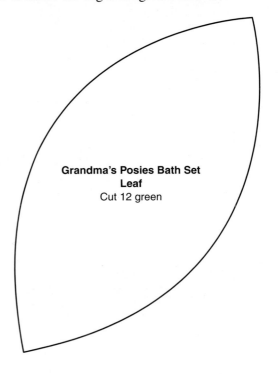

Grandma's Posies Bath Set
Leaf
Cut 12 green

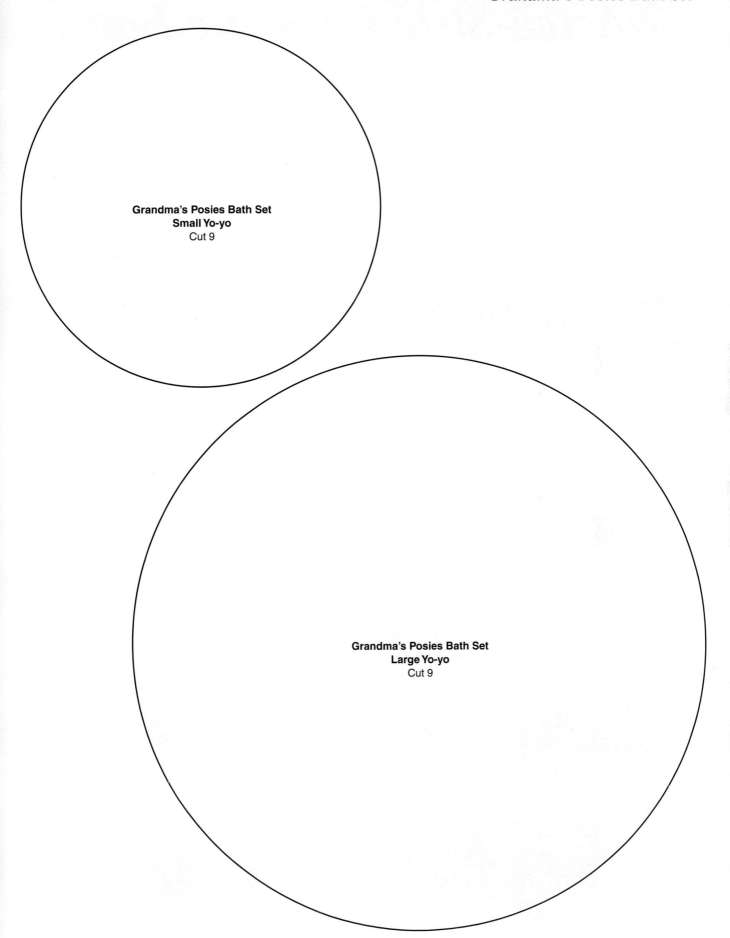

**Grandma's Posies Bath Set
Small Yo-yo**
Cut 9

**Grandma's Posies Bath Set
Large Yo-yo**
Cut 9

Aztec-Style Cosmetic Bag and Glasses Case

By June Fiechter

Add a little trim to a commercial pattern to give some ethnic flavor and zing to a basic design.

Project Specifications

Skill Level: Beginner

Cosmetic Bag Size: Approximately 6" x 7¾" x 4½"

Eye Glasses Case Size: 3¾" x 6¾"

Materials

- Simplicity Crafts Pattern #7098
- Tan and brown textured fabrics to total amount designated by pattern
- Turquoise lining fabric in amount designated by pattern
- All-purpose thread to match fabrics including black and dark brown
- 14 (7mm) turquoise floral rings
- 14 (4mm) round black beads
- 7 (18mm x 6mm) Aztec sun pendants
- Fusible batting as designated on pattern
- Black zipper in size designated on pattern
- Basic sewing supplies and tools

Instructions

Cosmetic Bag

Step 1. Cut out bag pieces, splicing a 5½" (plus seam allowance) width of brown fabric in center of bag body front as shown in photo. Repeat for a bag body back.

Step 2. Fuse batting to pattern pieces and line with turquoise lining fabric. Machine-quilt grid on layered bag pieces with straight stitch and dark brown thread. Mark Aztec pattern on band pieces for top of bag and stitch with black thread and tiny zigzag stitch.

Step 3. Finish bag following pattern instructions.

Step 4. Referring to photo for placement, sew one Aztec sun pendant in the center of each diamond in Aztec band pattern. On each side of pendants, where

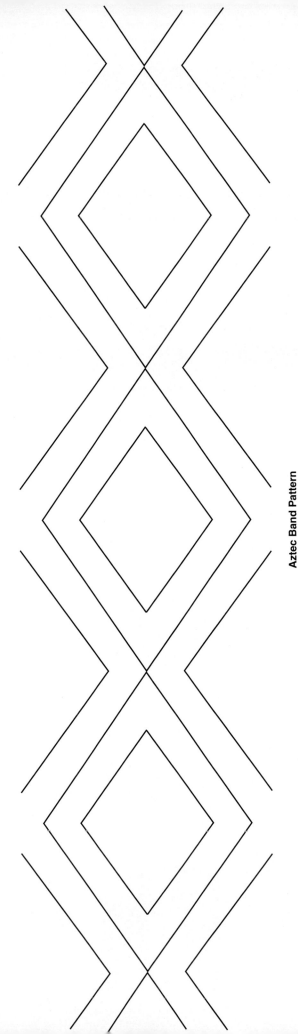

Aztec Band Pattern

X's are formed by stitching, sew a round black bead and a turquoise floral ring. The turquoise floral ring will be held in place by the round black bead.

Eye Glasses Case

Step 1. Cut eye glasses case fabrics, lining and fusible batting as instructed on commercial pattern; fuse as instructed. Layer pieces.

Step 2. Machine-quilt grid on eye glasses case pieces with straight stitch and dark brown thread.

Step 3. Finish eye glasses case following pattern instructions.

Step 4. Referring to photo for placement sew one Aztec sun pendant in center front of tan band. Position six turquoise floral rings and six black beads along upper edge of tan band. Sewing black bead in place will secure turquoise floral ring. ✂

Ribbons & Roses Tote Bag

Continued from page 52

match heart shape. Sew burgundy bias tape over lower raw edges of heart side seams to point.

Step 4. Place bag front and back on lining pieces and trim to shape. Wrong sides together, baste lining to bag front and back. Bind top edges of heart. Do not bind along side seams.

Step 5. From natural canvas and burgundy print cut one gusset piece each 2" x 36". Wrong sides together, baste around the edges.

Step 6. Find lower bag center front and center back and mark with pins. Find center of gusset. Matching centers, sew gusset to front and back sections of bag with raw edges exposed on the outside. Bind edges with burgundy bias tape.

Step 7. Cut two canvas strips 2" x 18" for handles. Fold raw edges to the center and press. Cover raw edges with bias tape and topstitch down each side.

Step 8. Attach handles to top of bag referring to photo for placement.

Step 9. Make two bows from burgundy bias tape and sew to point of heart front and back, referring to photo for placement. Hot-glue ribbon roses at ends of handles, on bows and down front and back of bag. ✂

The Nursery

Let's face it—babies take a long time to get here! What better way to make use of this time than to get out your fabric scraps and sew something ever-so-special for the precious little one for whom you're so patiently waiting?

Our soft and fluffy hooded bath towels will keep baby warm and dry after bath time; and our friendly bear diaper stacker and car seat cover will give you and your little tot lots of warm smiles.

You'll find page after page of great baby gift ideas that are sure to please your special little someone—and his or her mom!

Fuzzy Bunny Blanket

By Chris Malone

This easy-to-make, soft-as-down blanket is bound to become baby's naptime favorite.

Project Specifications

Skill Level: Beginner

Blanket Size: Approximately 36" x 36"

Materials

- 1 yard pink plush felt
- 9" x 12" white plush felt
- Tiny scrap of white or pink felt or fleece
- White, medium and light green, medium and light blue, medium and light pink and yellow 6-strand embroidery floss
- 4¾ yards pink satin blanket binding
- White quilting or buttonhole thread
- Pink all-purpose thread to match blanket binding
- Air-soluble marker
- Embroidery needle
- Fabric glue
- Basic sewing supplies and tools

Instructions

Step 1. From pink plush felt cut a square 36" x 36". Cut bunny from white plush felt.

Step 2. For bunny's eye, cut a ¼" circle of white or pink felt or fleece. Position and glue in place. With 4 strands of medium pink embroidery floss, satin-stitch over circle to cover.

Step 3. Referring to photo for placement, pin bunny on one edge of pink plush square. Bunny legs should be 5" from bottom of square.

Step 4. Referring to photo, use air-soluble marker to draw a gently curving line 5"–7" from bottom edge of square. Raise bunny to continue line behind legs. Start and stop line 1¾" from sides of square. You may need to press firmly to mark on plush.

Step 5. With 4 strands of medium green embroidery floss, use outline stitch to cover ground line.

Step 6. Referring to photo, sketch leaves, stems and flowers on each side of bunny. Outline-stitch stems with medium green and leaves with 4 strands light green embroidery floss.

Step 7. For flowers, use 4 strands of medium blue or medium pink floss to make eight lazy-daisy stitches ½" long radiating from a common center. With lighter shade of each color, make another eight lazy-daisy stitches ⁵⁄₁₆" long with each stitch between a longer stitch of the same color. Make a blue and a pink flower each side of the bunny. Make three or four yellow French knots in the center of each flower.

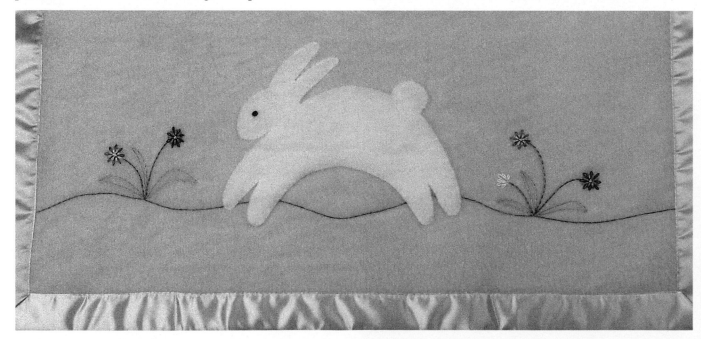

Step 8. On right side of bunny, make half of a white flower by making four longer lazy-daisy stitches with a shorter lazy-daisy stitch on each side. Make four yellow French knots at base of white flower (see Sewing Guidelines on page 173).

Step 9. Sew bunny to background with white quilting or buttonhole thread and a small appliqué stitch.

Step 10. Bind square, mitering corners, with blanket binding.

Note: If binding is prefolded off-center, the narrow side is aligned with raw edge of blanket. If binding puckers, experiment with stitch tension. ✄

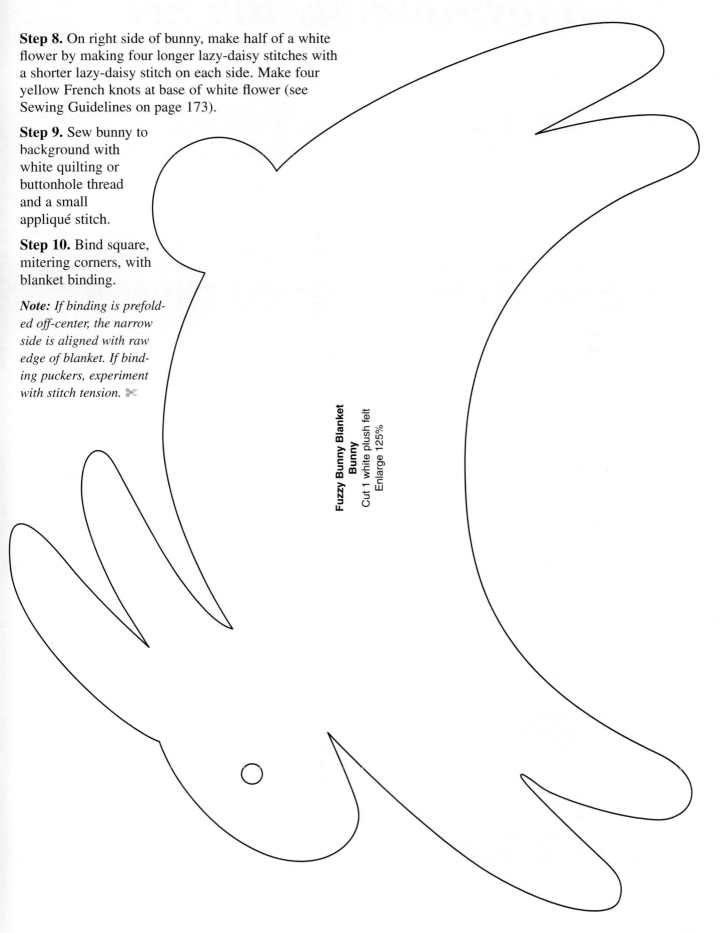

Fuzzy Bunny Blanket Bunny
Cut 1 white plush felt
Enlarge 125%

Baby Animals Bib Set

By Julie Weaver

Because chenille is so soft, cuddly and washable, it's a natural for babies (and busy moms).

Project Specifications

Skill Level: Beginner

Bib Size: Fits any size

Materials

Note: Materials are for one bib. If same fabric color is selected for both, two bibs can be made from ⅓ yard chenille and ⅛ yard ribbing. Scraps for appliqué may vary by preference.

- ⅓ yard chenille
- ⅛ yard matching cotton ribbing
- 2 yards matching wide single-fold bias tape
- Scraps of fusible transfer web
- Variety of scraps for appliqué
- 6" x 6" fabric stabilizer
- All-purpose threads to match fabrics
- Contrasting threads for machine-appliqué
- Water-soluble marker
- Black 6-strand embroidery floss for pig
- Pink and gray 6-strand embroidery floss for bunny
- 2 (¼") black buttons for eyes
- Basic sewing supplies and tools

Instructions

Step 1. Cut a 12" x 18" piece of chenille.

Step 2. Unfold single-fold bias tape and finger-press a ¼" hem at one end. Pin one edge of bias tape to wrong side of chenille rectangle, starting with finger-pressed hem at center of one short end (back of bib). Using the fold of the bias tape as a guide, stitch to chenille, mitering corners and overlapping at center back. Turn tape to front, pin miters at corners and topstitch in place.

Step 3. Fold top edge of bib down to back 6" and use pattern to cut neck opening as shown in Fig. 1. Stay-stitch the neck opening.

Step 4. Cut a piece of cotton ribbing 2¼" x 14½". Sew short ends together. With wrong sides together, fold ribbing in

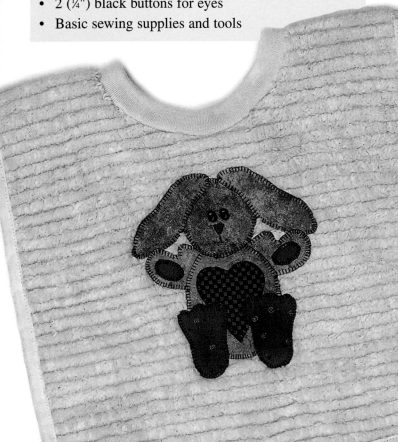

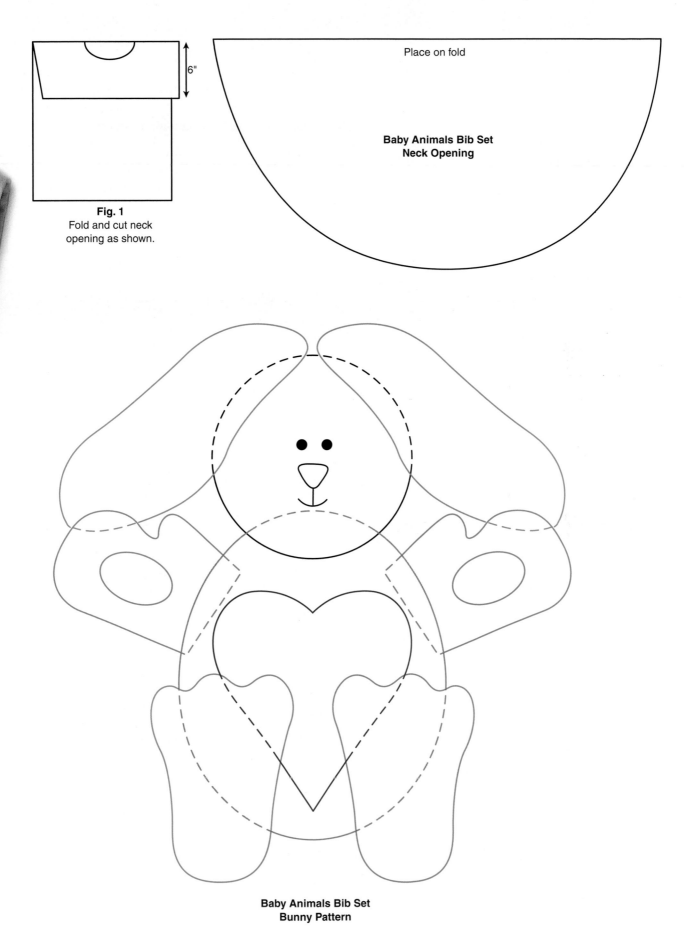

Fig. 1
Fold and cut neck
opening as shown.

6"

Place on fold

**Baby Animals Bib Set
Neck Opening**

**Baby Animals Bib Set
Bunny Pattern**

half lengthwise; press. Divide neck opening and ribbing in four equal parts and mark with water-soluble marker. Folded, and with right sides together, pin ribbing to neck, matching segment marks. Stitch ribbing in place, easing fullness if necessary.

Step 5. Trace appliqué shapes for selected design on paper side of fusible transfer web as directed on patterns. Cut out leaving roughly ¼" margin around traced lines. Following manufacturer's instructions, fuse to selected fabric scraps. Cut out on traced lines.

Step 6. Referring to photo and pattern of choice for placement, center pieces 1" down from bottom of ribbed neck edge; fuse.

Step 7. Pin fabric stabilizer behind design area. With contrasting thread, machine-appliqué around each piece with satin or buttonhole stitch.

Step 8. On baby pig, use 3 strands of black embroidery floss to embroider two French knots on snout as shown on pattern. Use water-soluble marker to draw nose and mouth on bunny. Use 3 strands of pink embroidery floss to satin-stitch the nose. Use 3 strands of gray floss to backstitch the mouth. ✂

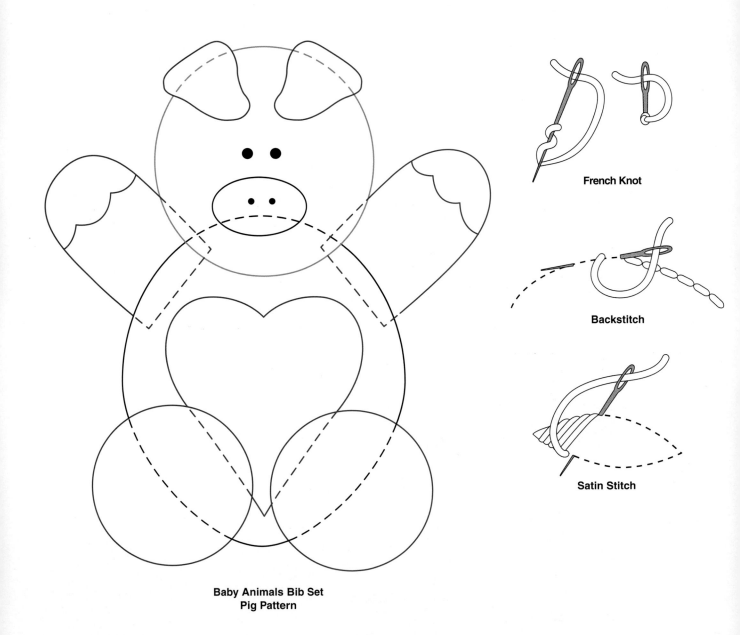

French Knot

Backstitch

Satin Stitch

**Baby Animals Bib Set
Pig Pattern**

Baby Ducky Onesie

By Julie Weaver

This little one-piece garment has become such a practical infant-wear item.
With a few scraps and a tiny bit of time, practical can also be mighty cute!

Project Specifications

Skill Level: Beginner

Size: Infant size of choice

Materials

- Purchased onesie
- Orange and yellow scraps for appliqué
- Scraps of fusible transfer web
- All-purpose threads to match fabrics
- 6" x 6" fabric stabilizer
- 2 (¼") black buttons
- 6-strand yellow embroidery floss
- Basic sewing supplies and tools

Instructions

Step 1. Trace appliqué shapes on paper side of fusible transfer web as directed on patterns. Cut out leaving roughly ¼" margin around traced lines.

Step 2. Following manufacturer's instructions, fuse shapes to selected fabric scraps. Cut out on traced lines.

Step 3. Referring to photo and pattern, arrange pieces on front of onesie, approximately 1" down from neck and centered on front; fuse.

Step 4. Pin fabric stabilizer behind design area. With matching threads, machine-appliqué around shapes with buttonhole or satin stitch. Use smaller stitch size around bill.

Step 5. Sew buttons in place for eyes. Use 3 strands of yellow embroidery floss to chain-stitch feathers on top of head. ✂

Continued on page 68

Bath Time Fun Hooded Towels

By Janice Loewenthal

*Stop those tears! Slip the towel hood over baby's head
to stop the inevitable dribbles that ruin all the fun.*

Project Specifications

Skill Level: Beginner

Hooded Towel Size: Bath towel size of choice

Materials

Note: Materials are for one towel.

- 1 purchased bath towel
- 1 matching washcloth
- ¼ yard fabric for binding
- Scraps of fabric for appliqué
- Scraps of fusible transfer web
- Scraps of fabric stabilizer
- All-purpose threads to match or contrast with fabrics
- Basic sewing supplies and tools

Instructions

Note: Appliqué designs are included for three different towels.

Step 1. Cut four 1½" strips across width of binding fabric. Join end to end to make binding. Press seams open.

Step 2. Cut washcloth diagonally slightly larger than half to allow for seam allowance. Cut a strip of binding 2" longer than diagonal measurement. Right sides together, center, align raw edges and stitch as shown in Fig. 1; press. Turn under ¼" along outer raw edge and stitch. Fold to back side and stitch by hand or machine.

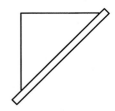

Fig. 1
Align binding with diagonal edge of hood as shown.

Step 3. Trace appliqué shapes of choice on paper side

of fusible transfer web. Cut out leaving roughly ¼" around traced lines. Fuse, following manufacturer's instructions, to selected fabrics. Cut out on traced lines.

Step 4. Referring to photo, arrange appliqués on hood and fuse.

Step 5. Pin a piece of fabric stabilizer slightly larger than design area on reverse side of hood. Satin-stitch around appliqué shapes and on detail lines. Clip threads and remove stabilizer.

Step 6. Pin or baste hood to corner of towel as shown in Fig. 2. Trim excess binding from edge of hood.

Step 7. Align raw edge of binding strip with outer edge of towel, beginning at center bottom. Stitch around perimeter and join ends with a seam; press. Turn under ¼" along outer raw edge and stitch. Fold to backside of towel and stitch by hand or machine.

Step 8. Repeat with all three designs for three times the fun! ✂

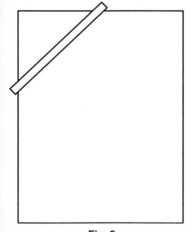

Fig. 2
Place hood on corner
of towel as shown.

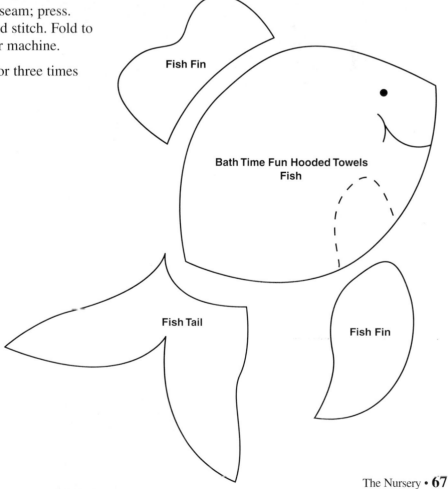

Fish Fin

**Bath Time Fun Hooded Towels
Fish**

Fish Tail

Fish Fin

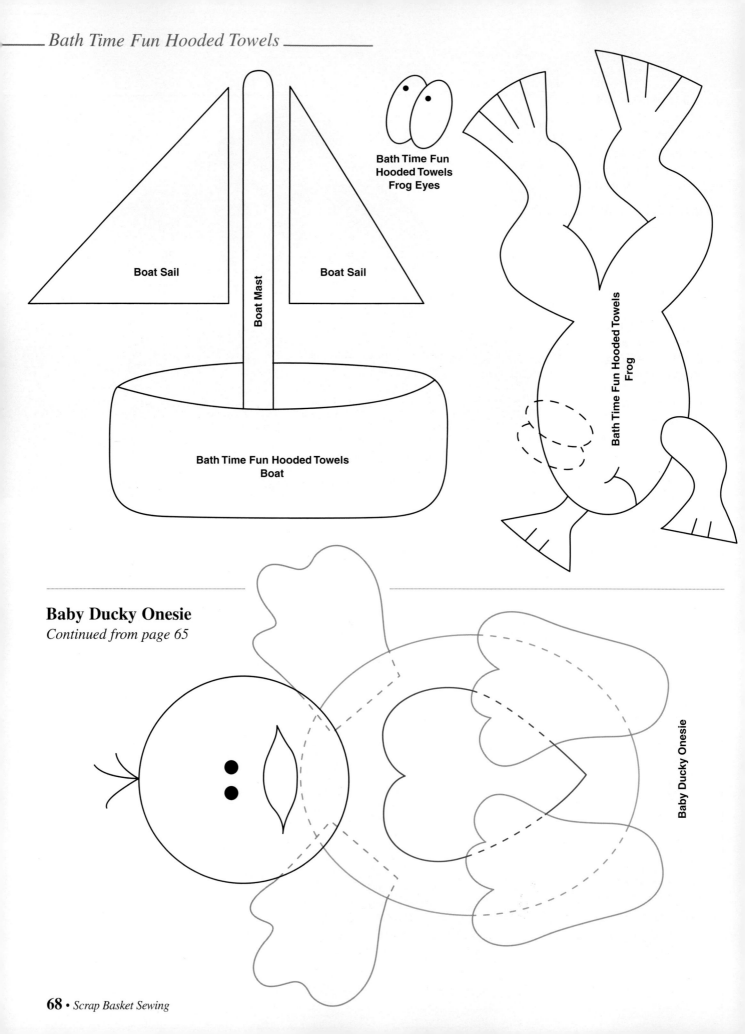

Boat Sail

Boat Mast

Boat Sail

Bath Time Fun Hooded Towels Frog Eyes

Bath Time Fun Hooded Towels Boat

Bath Time Fun Hooded Towels Frog

Baby Ducky Onesie
Continued from page 65

Baby Ducky Onesie

Baby Tote

By Marian Shenk

*Make a carryall for baby with plenty of cargo space
and enough outside pockets to stash all the necessaries.*

Project Specifications

Skill Level: Beginner

Tote Bag Size: Approximately 13½" x 14" x 3"

Materials

- ¾ yard denim
- ½ yard lining fabric
- Scraps of navy, medium blue, yellow, orange, medium brown and beige for appliqué
- 2 (¾") yellow buttons
- Scraps of fusible transfer web
- 6" (¼"-wide) yellow satin ribbon
- ¾" x 1" piece hook-and-loop tape
- Clear nylon monofilament
- All-purpose threads to match fabrics
- 6-strand black embroidery floss
- Basic sewing supplies and tools

Instructions

Step 1. From denim fabric cut two bag pieces 17½" x 17½" and one pocket piece 8" x 17½". From lining fabric cut two bag pieces 15" x 17½" and one packet piece 7" x 17½".

Step 2. Right sides together, align one long edge of pocket lining with one long edge of denim pocket and stitch. Align other long edge of pocket and lining, wrong sides together; press.

Step 3. Trace appliqué shapes on paper side of fusible transfer web as directed on patterns. Cut out leaving roughly ¼" margin around traced lines. Following manufacturer's instructions, fuse to selected fabrics. Cut out on traced lines.

Step 4. Referring to photo, fuse shapes to pocket. With clear nylon monofilament, satin-stitch around appliqués.

Step 5. Sew the ¾" yellow buttons to the baby carriage for wheels. Tie a yellow satin ribbon bow and stitch to teddy bear's neck. With 2 strands of black embroidery floss, stitch eyes and face on duck and teddy bear.

Step 6. Place pocket right side up on right side of bag front, aligning lower bag edges. Sew sides and lower edge of pocket to bag front. Divide pocket in three equal vertical sections and sew top to bottom through all layers.

Step 7. Trace letters on paper side of fusible transfer web and fuse to bag front as in Steps 3 and 4 above.

Step 8. Right sides together, align one 17½" edge of lining with top edge of bag front and stitch. Align other 17½" edge of bag front and lining, wrong sides together; press. Repeat for bag back and lining.

Step 9. Place bag front and back right sides together and stitch sides and across bottom of all layers except back lining. Bring back lining down over stitched bag and sew around leaving a 5" opening at the bottom. Turn right side out and close opening with hand stitches.

Step 10. Pull corners out to align bottom seam with side seams. Stitch a 3" seam across points to form bag bottom as shown in Fig. 1.

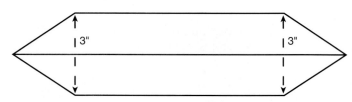

Fig. 1
Stitch across bag bottom as shown.

Step 11. Cut two strips 2" x 32" from denim for straps. Fold in half lengthwise and stitch long edges of each. Turn right side out and press seam down center back of strap. Fold raw edges into ends of straps. Pin to front and back of bag 3" in from side seams. Topstitch in place with an X as shown in Fig. 2.

Step 12. Cut a piece of denim 2½" x 4". Fold in half lengthwise and sew long edges. Round off one end as

**Baby Tote
Letter B
Cut 2 navy**

**Baby Tote
Letter A
Cut 1 navy**

**Baby Tote
Letter Y
Cut 1 navy**

shown in Fig. 3. Turn right side out and center seam down back of tube. Fold raw ends to inside. Stitch straight end to inside center of bag's back top edge with X as shown in Fig. 2.

Step 13. Sew hook-and-loop tape to fastener tab and center front of bag. ✄

Fig. 2
Stitch with X as shown.

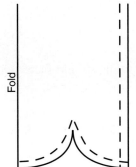

Fig. 3
Round ends of fastener as shown.

**Baby Tote
Teddy Bear**
Cut 1 medium brown

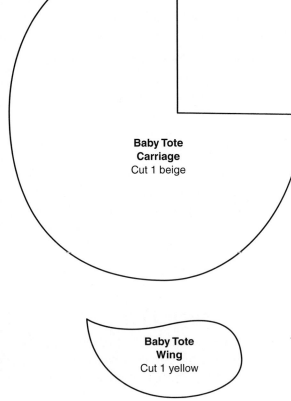

**Baby Tote
Carriage**
Cut 1 beige

**Baby Tote
Duck Bill**
Cut 1 orange

**Baby Tote
Duck**
Cut 1 yellow

**Baby Tote
Wing**
Cut 1 yellow

**Baby Tote
Puddle**
Cut 1 medium blue

Berry Special
Baby Bib & Burp Pad

By Nancy Billetdeaux

Make this "berry special" set for "berry special" occasions.
It is so crisp and pretty it will make any baby outfit extra-special.

Project Specifications

Skill Level: Beginner

Burp Pad Size: Approximately 10" x 22"

Bib Size: Approximately 10" x 8¾"

Materials

- ¼ yard white prequilted fabric
- ½ yard red print fabric
- Scraps of green print fabric
- 4 (⅜") white buttons
- All-purpose white thread
- Red 6-strand embroidery floss
- Scraps of fusible transfer web
- Basic sewing supplies and tools

Instructions

Bib

Step 1. Trace and cut bib as directed on pattern.

Step 2. From red print fabric cut 61 squares 3" x 3" for prairie points and two strips 2" x 12" for ties.

Step 3. Fold each 3" x 3" square in half, wrong sides together. To make a prairie point, bring left and right folded corners up to center until side is even with the top as shown in Fig. 1. Fold left and right corners to center and pin as shown in Fig. 2. Nineteen prairie points will be used for bib. Put aside 42 prairie points for burp pad.

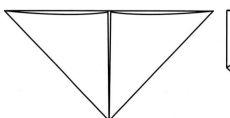

Fig. 1
Bring left and right folded
corners to center as shown.

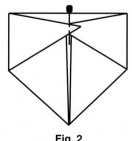

Fig. 2
Bring left and right corners
to center and pin.

Step 4. Fold one bib section (back) in half and pin to mark centers. Pin 17 prairie points to right side of bib back, starting at center. Continue around bib, stopping about ⅜" from shoulder. Raw edges of prairie points should be aligned with raw edges of bib. Unfolded sides of prairie points should face right side of bib. Stitch in place with ¼" seam allowance.

Step 5. Trace words on front bib section. With 2 strands of red embroidery floss, outline-stitch the words.

Step 6. Referring to photo, pin two remaining prairie points to front of bib. With machine, satin-stitch across raw edges.

Step 7. Trace strawberry leaves on paper side of fusible transfer web as instructed on pattern. Cut out leaving roughly ¼" margin around traced lines. Following manufacturer's instructions, fuse to selected fabrics.

Step 8. Referring to photo, place leaves on prairie points; fuse. Sew white buttons to strawberries.

Step 9. Fold one 2" x 12" red print strip in half lengthwise, wrong sides together; press. Open strip and fold outer edges to center fold, wrong sides facing; press. Press center fold again and fold one short end in. Stitch close to folded edges and across folded end. Repeat for second tie.

Step 10. Align raw end of each tie with raw edge of shoulder seam on one bib section ⅜" from neck edge. Place both bib sections together, right sides facing, and stitch around bib with ⅜" seam allowance, leaving small section open for turning.

Step 11. Turn bib right side out and close opening with hand stitches.

Burp Pad

Step 1. From white prequilted fabric cut two rectangles 9" x 21½". Round the corners of each using rounded corner of bib pattern as a guide. Mark the center of each side of one rectangle.

Step 2. Pin a prairie point to each marked center point. Raw edges of prairie points should be aligned with raw edges of rectangle. Unfolded sides of prairie points should face right side of rectangle. Pin the rest of the prairie points (reserve two) along the sides and ends adjusting when necessary by bringing the sides of the prairie points in more or less. Stitch in place using ¼" seam allowance.

Step 3. Trace words on remaining rectangle. Embroider and appliqué as in Bib Steps 4–7.

Step 4. Place two rectangles together, right sides facing. Stitch around perimeter with ⅜" seam allowance, leaving small opening for turning.

Step 5. Turn right side out and close opening with hand stitches. ✂

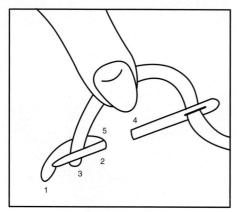

Embroidery Stitch Diagram
Bring needle up at 1. Keep the thread above the stitches, go down at 2 and come up at 3. Go down at 4 and come up at 5.

Berry Special Baby Bib & Burp Pad
Strawberry Leaves
Cut 4 green print

Berry Special Baby Burp Pad
Lettering Pattern for Burp Pad

Have A "Berry" Nice Day !

Berry Special Baby Bib
Bib Pattern
Cut 2 white prequilted fabric
Enlarge 115%

Cuddle Buddies Baby Car Seat Cover & Diaper Stacker

By Pearl Louise Krush

Keep baby soft and warm with this cleverly designed car seat cover. Stack disposable diapers near at hand, but out of the way and under disguise, to keep baby's nursery cute and functional.

Project Specifications

Skill Level: Beginner

Car Seat Cover Size: Newborn car seat size

Diaper Stacker Size: 10" x 19" x 7"

Materials

- 2⅔ yards pastel flannel
- 1⅓ yards thin cotton batting
- ⅓ yard blue plaid flannel for bows
- ¼ yard brown chenille
- 2 scraps of black felt
- 4 (½") black buttons
- 4 (1") pastel heart buttons
- Polyester fiberfill
- All-purpose threads to match fabrics, including black
- Pattern paper 22" x 32"
- 50" (¼"-wide) elastic
- Small safety pin
- 7" x 10" firm cardboard
- Cool-temperature glue gun
- Basic sewing supplies and tools

Instructions

Diaper Stacker

Step 1. From pastel flannel cut a rectangle 20" x 36". Fold in half, right sides together, bringing 20" edges together. Sew a ½" seam, starting at one end and extending 6" as shown in Fig. 1. Turn under ¼" twice on each side of remainder of 20" length and stitch for hems.

Step 2. Place hemmed edges right sides together and sew a 3" seam as shown in Fig. 2.

Step 3. Right sides together, fold the bag with the seam down the center back. Sew across the bottom of the bag. Flatten the bottom seam with the points of the bottom pulled to the outside as shown in Fig. 3. Sew across the points 3½" from each point to form a boxed bottom for the bag.

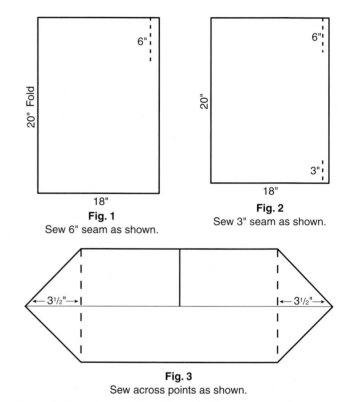

Fig. 1
Sew 6" seam as shown.

Fig. 2
Sew 3" seam as shown.

Fig. 3
Sew across points as shown.

Step 4. Turn bag right side out. Finger-pleat the top in 1½"–2" pleats on each side until the top of the bag measures 3". Sew a stay-stitch seam across pleats to hold in place.

Step 5. Cut bear head, nose and ears as directed on pattern. Referring to pattern and photo, pin nose in place. With 2 strands of black all-purpose thread, sew nose to head front with buttonhole stitch. Backstitch muzzle and mouth.

Step 6. Place two ear pieces right sides together. Stitch around curve, leaving end open. Clip curve and turn right side out. Repeat for two ears.

Step 7. Place ears on head front as indicated on pattern, aligning raw edges. Place head back on head front, right sides together. Sew around edges, leaving neck open. Clip seams and turn right side out. Stuff firmly with polyester fiberfill. Sew two black button eyes in place pulling thread tightly for indentation.

Step 8. Insert bag top into bear neck opening. Sew in place with hand stitches.

Step 9. From blue plaid flannel cut a strip 2" x 8". Fold the strip lengthwise, right sides together; stitch long edge. Turn right side out and fold raw edges of ends in and stitch. Fold one short end of strip over other short end and sew 1¼" up from neck to back of bear head for hanging loop.

Step 10. From blue plaid flannel cut a 6" strip across the width of the fabric. Fold in half lengthwise, right sides together. Sew long edge, leaving 3" opening in center for turning. Stitch diagonally across ends and trim seams. Turn right side out; press. Loop pieces to form bow shape and streamers.

Step 11. From blue plaid flannel cut a rectangle 5" x 6". Fold in half lengthwise, stitch and turn right side out. Center seam at back of tube and press. Wrap around center of looped bow, overlapping ends on the back of bow. Sew ends with hand stitches and sew bow below bear head.

Step 12. From pastel flannel cut a rectangle 9" x 12". Center the 7" x 10" firm cardboard on the wrong side of flannel. Place a small amount of glue at each cardboard corner and pull fabric corners into the glue. Glue remaining fabric edges to back of cardboard. Insert covered cardboard in bottom of diaper stacker to finish.

Car Seat Cover

Step 1. Round corners of 22" x 32" pattern paper to make an oval. Using oval pattern cut two shapes from pastel flannel and one from thin batting. Place two flannel pieces, right sides together, on top of batting. Pin-baste layers together.

Step 2. Use inner dashed line of peek-a-boo pattern to cut opening in layered flannel and batting. Center opening 8" from top of oval as shown in Fig. 4.

Step 3. Sew around outer edges of layered flannel oval,

leaving 1" opening to insert elastic. Turn right side out through peek-a-boo opening. Stitch around oval ¾" from seam to form casing.

Step 4. From blue plaid flannel cut a 2½" strip across the width of the fabric. Fold lengthwise, wrong sides together. Fold one short end in ½". Sew raw edges of folded binding to raw edges of peek-a-boo opening, right sides together. Tuck raw short end into folded end. Bring folded edges of binding to inside of peek-a-boo opening and hand-stitch in place.

Step 5. Cut peek-a-boo lid as directed on pattern. Place flannel pieces, right sides together, on batting piece. Sew around perimeter, leaving 3" opening for turning. Turn right side out and close opening with hand stitches.

Step 6. Make bear head as in Diaper Stacker Steps 5–7, using flannel for head back. Do not stuff. Close neck opening with hand stitches. Referring to photo, hand-sew to peek-a-boo lid.

Step 7. From blue plaid flannel cut one rectangle each 6½" x 8" and 5" x 6". Fold the larger rectangle in half lengthwise, right sides together. Sew around perimeter, leaving 2" opening. Turn right side out; press.

Step 8. Fold smaller rectangle in half lengthwise, wrong sides together. Stitch long side and turn right side out. Center seam at back; press. Wrap around larger flannel rectangle and stitch ends together in back to form bow. Referring to photo for placement, sew below bear head.

Step 9. Insert safety pin in one end of ¼"-wide elastic and thread through casing around oval. Fasten ends together and let ends slip inside opening. Close opening with hand stitches.

Step 10. Attach peek-a-boo lid to oval with four heart-shaped buttons as shown in photo. ✂

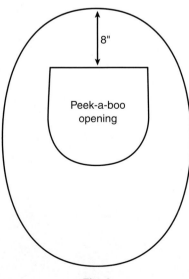

Fig. 4
Cut peek-a-boo opening
as shown.

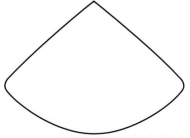

Cuddle Buddies
Baby Car Seat Cover & Diaper Stacker
Bear Nose
Cut 2 black felt

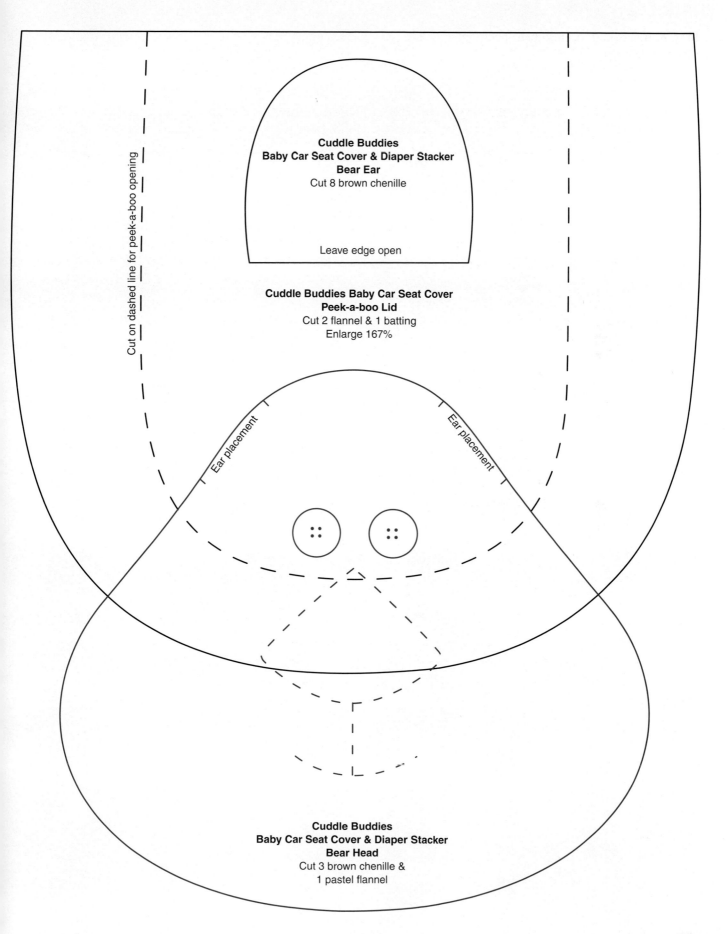

**Cuddle Buddies
Baby Car Seat Cover & Diaper Stacker
Bear Ear**
Cut 8 brown chenille

Leave edge open

**Cuddle Buddies Baby Car Seat Cover
Peek-a-boo Lid**
Cut 2 flannel & 1 batting
Enlarge 167%

Cut on dashed line for peek-a-boo opening

Ear placement

Ear placement

**Cuddle Buddies
Baby Car Seat Cover & Diaper Stacker
Bear Head**
Cut 3 brown chenille &
1 pastel flannel

The Kid's Room

This chapter is chock-full of projects for kids from 2 to 20! Search through your scraps for the most colorful ones to use in these fun projects!

Your little ones will enjoy hours of fun playing with our Noah's Ark play mat and finger puppets or the chubby, fleecy lamb. Preschoolers will proudly carry their markers and crayons in colorful totes. Older kids will enjoy Noah's Ark puppets in Sunday school. And teens will appreciate accessories made for their rooms from recycled jeans.

What are you waiting for? Get stitching!

Denim Duo Dorm Set

By Pattie Donham

The denim look is perfect for decorating and personalizing student rooms.
And Mom should be really happy—recycled jeans are easy on the pocketbook!

Project Specifications

Skill Level: Beginner

Lamp Shade Size: Any size

Ball Size: 45" circumference

Materials

For Ball

- Laundered and pressed recycled denim jeans
- Large package of polyester fiberfill

For Lamp Shade

- Laundered and pressed recycled denim jeans (amount will vary with size of lamp shade)
- Lamp shade of choice
- Newspaper for pattern tracing
- Spring clothespins
- Hot-glue gun

For Both Projects

- Temporary marker
- All-purpose thread to match fabric
- Basic sewing supplies and tools

Instructions

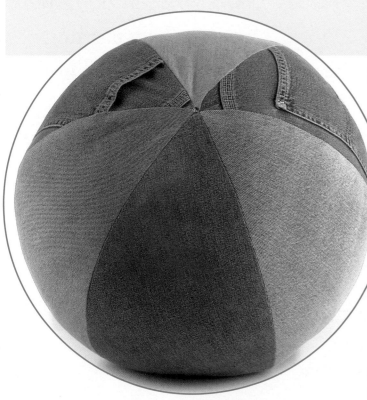

Ball

Step 1. Trace and cut pieces as directed on pattern, adding ⅝" seam allowance on curved outer edges.

Step 2. With ⅝" seam allowance, sew two pieces together, right sides facing. Backstitch several stitches at each pointed end. Repeat with all six pieces, joining the first to the last to form a ball shape. Leave an opening in the final seam for turning and stuffing.

Step 3. Turn ball right side out and stuff firmly with polyester fiberfill. Close opening with hand stitches.

Lamp Shade

Step 1. Place newspaper on work surface. Place lamp shade on its side on newspaper. Starting at shade seam, trace around top and bottom as you slowly roll the shade back to the seam.

Step 2. Fold the traced pattern into thirds and cut on fold lines to make three pattern pieces. Identify the cut sides of the pattern, which will later be rejoined.

Step 3. Cut and/or open seams of recycled jeans as necessary and pin pattern pieces in place. Cut out pieces allowing ⅝" seam allowance on all sides of pattern.

Step 4. With ⅝" seam allowance, sew pieces together at identified sides, right sides facing, to form a cone shape. Turn right side out.

Step 5. Place denim cover over lamp shade and smooth out any wrinkles. Hot-glue denim to top and bottom inside edges of shade. Hold glued edges in place with spring clothespins, but remove immediately when glue dries. ✂

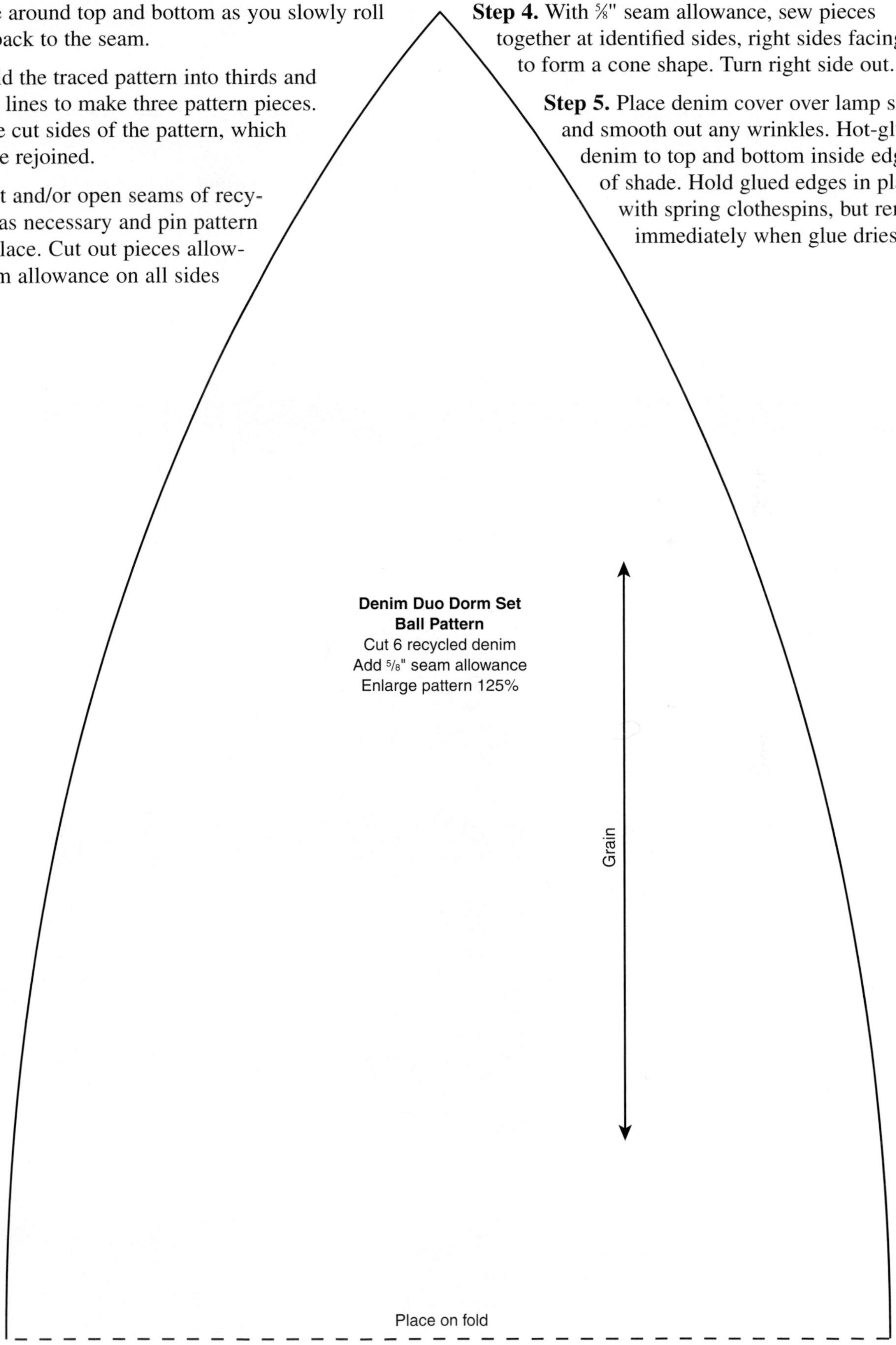

**Denim Duo Dorm Set
Ball Pattern**
Cut 6 recycled denim
Add ⅝" seam allowance
Enlarge pattern 125%

Grain

Place on fold

Yo-Yo Tic-Tac-Toe Game

By Mary Ayres

*With a few scraps and minimal sewing time you can make a
very entertaining and portable game for use at home or in travel.*

Project Specifications

Skill Level: Beginner

Game Size: Approximately 9" x 9"

Materials

- 9½" x 9½" solid or textured fabric square for top of game board
- Two 9½" x 5¾" fabric pieces for game board backing
- Five 4" circles each of two different fabrics for playing pieces
- Thin batting square 9½" x 9½"
- 2¼ yards black jumbo rickrack
- Basic sewing supplies and tools

Instructions

Step 1. On the right side, mark a line 3¼" in from each edge of 9½" solid or textured fabric game board fabric square.

Step 2. Baste batting square to reverse side of 9½" game board fabric square.

Step 3. Cut four 9½" pieces of black jumbo rickrack. Sew one piece on each marked line, stitching through the center of rickrack.

Step 4. Sew remaining piece of black jumbo rickrack around all four edges of game board fabric square ¼" from edge, starting and stopping at a corner.

Step 5. Turn one long edge of each game board backing piece under ¼"; press. Turn under ¼" again. Stitch close to edge.

Step 6. Pin backing pieces to game board front, right sides together and hemmed edges of backing overlapped. Sew front to back along previous rickrack stitching. Trim corners, turn right side out and press.

Step 7. Sew a basting stitch around the edge of each 4" fabric circle, turning fabric under ⅛" and gathering as you sew. Pull basting stitches up tightly and knot thread ends to secure. Flatten circles to make yo-yo playing pieces.

Step 8. Store yo-yo playing pieces inside game board when not in use. ✄

Chunky Colors Tote Set

By Holly Daniels

Whether made for traveling in the car or just keeping things orderly at home, these organizers for crayons and markers are a nifty idea.

Project Specifications

Skill Level: Beginner

Tote Size: Approximately 8½" x 13"

Crayon Roll Size: Approximately 7" x 9" (open)

Materials

Note: Crayon pockets are designed for large crayons and markers. If using smaller crayons, adjust the size of pockets to 2" x 4½". All other instructions remain the same.

For Crayon Roll

- ¼ yard bright crayon novelty print
- ¼ yard green plaid
- 1 fabric scrap each 2½" x 4½" of crayon colors red, blue, green, yellow, orange, purple, black and brown
- 1" x ¾" piece of hook-and-loop tape

- Thin batting or flannel 7" x 9"

For Tote

- ⅜ yard denim for tote
- ¼ yard green plaid
- 1 fabric scrap each 2½" x 4½" of crayon colors red, blue, green, yellow, orange, purple, black and brown
- 1½" x ¾" piece of hook-and-loop tape
- 26" piece of 1"-wide cotton webbing for tote straps
- 2 pieces thin batting or flannel 9" x 13½"

For Both Projects

- All-purpose thread to match fabrics
- Clear nylon monofilament
- Air-soluble marker
- Basic sewing supplies and tools

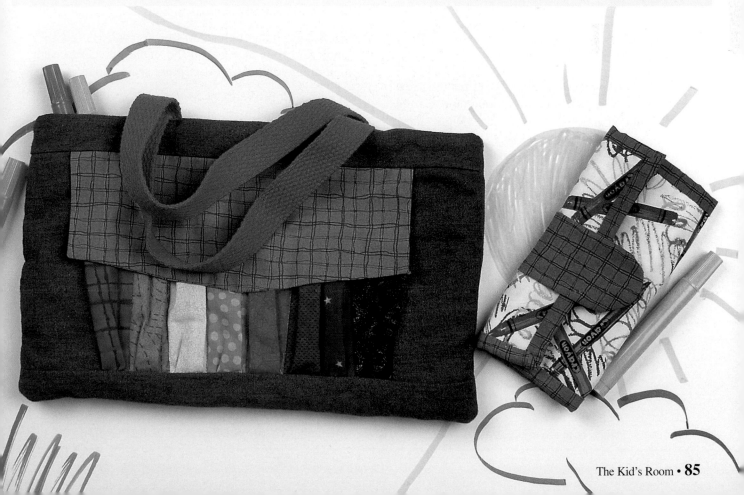

Instructions

Crayon Roll

Step 1. Arrange eight 2½" x 4½" crayon-colored fabric scraps in order desired. Stitch together on long sides and press seams open. Turn under one long edge of multicolored strip ¼" and topstitch with clear nylon monofilament in needle and neutral-colored thread in bobbin.

Step 2. From bright crayon novelty print cut two pieces 7" x 9". With air-soluble marker, mark one piece as shown in Fig. 1. Aligning seams of multicolored strip with marked lines, pin to marked piece. Create crayon pockets by stitching on all seam lines with matching thread or clear nylon monofilament. Baste sides and bottom edge to background piece, forming pleats at bottom edge.

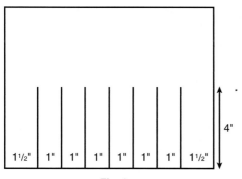

Fig. 1
Mark fabric strip as shown.

Step 3. Cut strap pieces as directed on pattern. Sew hook portion of 1" x ¾" hook-and-loop tape to right side of rounded end of one strap piece. Right sides together, sew around edges leaving short straight end open. Clip curve, turn right side out and press. Fold raw edges in ¼" and close opening with hand stitches.

Step 4. Sew loop portion of hook-and-loop tape to remaining 7" x 9" crayon novelty print piece cut in Step 2 as shown in Fig. 2.

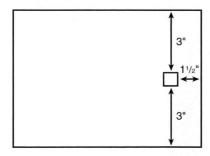

Fig. 2
Position hook-and-loop tape as shown.

Step 5. From bright crayon novelty print cut one piece 4" x 9" for inner flap. Turn under ¼" on one long edge and both short edges; topstitch to secure.

Step 6. Place outer piece prepared in Step 4 face down on work surface. Layer 7" x 9" batting or flannel piece between outer piece and pocket piece (right side up). Align inner flap, right side up, with top edge (not the pocket edge). Pin all layers in place.

Step 7. Cut a 2½" strip across the width of green plaid fabric for binding. Press in half lengthwise, wrong sides together. Bind perimeter of piece, catching top edge only of inner flap in bound edge.

Step 8. Insert crayons in pockets. Arrange inner flap over top of crayons and roll. Position strap so that hook-and-loop pieces match. Stitch straight end of strap in place with hand stitches.

Tote

Step 1. From denim cut one piece 6½" x 9". Prepare crayon pocket strip as in Crayon Roll, Step 1. Mark for sewing as in Step 2, but before stitching to denim, cut loop portion of hook-and-loop tape in half to make two squares ¾" x ¾". Sew one square of each ¼" from top edge of two center pockets. Continue to sew crayon pocket to marked denim as in Step 2 of Crayon Roll.

Step 2. From denim cut two pieces each 1¾" x 13½" and 2¾" x 6½". Sew one of the smaller pieces to each end of crayon pocket strip; press seams open.

Step 3. Cut pocket flaps as directed on pattern. Sew hook portion of hook-and-loop tape to one piece as shown on pattern. Pin flaps right sides together and stitch all edges except long straight edge. Turn right side out and press.

Step 4. Center and align pocket flap along top edge of crayon pocket, matching hook-and-loop pieces. Align one 1¾" x 13½" denim strip at top, right side facing pocket flap. Stitch and press seam open. Repeat with second strip at bottom of tote.

Step 5. From denim cut one piece 9" x 13½" for tote back. Cut two pieces the same size from green plaid for lining.

Step 6. Baste batting or flannel pieces to wrong sides of tote front and back. Mark the top of each 4½" from outer edges. Cut 1" cotton webbing in half to make two 13" straps. Pin one to front of tote, centering over marks. Repeat with second strip on tote back. Align raw edges of strips with raw edges of tote.

Step 7. Layer one lining piece with tote front, right sides together. Sew across top, catching handle in seam. Repeat with back.

Step 8. Layer tote lining pieces (front and back) right sides facing. Pin and sew on all three edges, leaving

6" opening for turning. Turn right side out and close opening with hand stitches.

Step 9. Tuck lining into tote. Secure corners with a tacking stitch. Topstitch close to top edge to hold lining in place. ✄

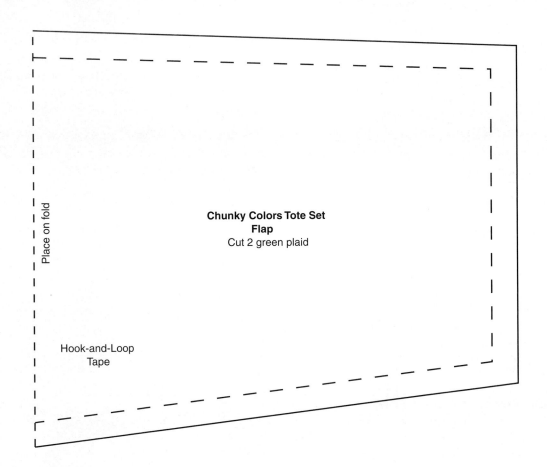

Place on fold

Chunky Colors Tote Set
Flap
Cut 2 green plaid

Hook-and-Loop
Tape

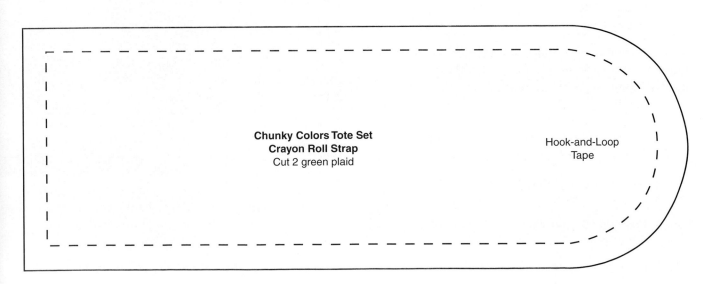

Chunky Colors Tote Set
Crayon Roll Strap
Cut 2 green plaid

Hook-and-Loop
Tape

Fresh as a Daisy Door Pillow

By Connie Matricardi

Great ID for a dorm room, camp or vacation cabin door—
even for personalizing the bedroom door at home.

Project Specifications

Skill Level: Beginner

Pillow Size: Approximately 7" x 7"

Materials

- 2 squares of gingham fabric 7½" x 7½"
- Four 7½"-long pieces white jumbo rickrack
- 1 square vinyl 3½" x 3½"
- 4 (¾") daisy buttons
- White all-purpose thread
- 3" x 3" photo
- 12" length of white cord
- Polyester fiberfill
- Basic sewing supplies and tools

Instructions

Step 1. Fold vinyl square to find center. Fold one length of jumbo rickrack to find center. Match centers and sew rickrack to vinyl as shown in Fig. 1.

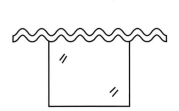

Fig. 1
Sew rickrack to vinyl
square as shown.

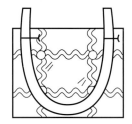

Fig. 2
Position cord on
pillow front as shown.

Step 2. Position vinyl square in center of one gingham square for pillow front. Pin rickrack ends to hold in place. Position and pin remaining lengths of rickrack so that they border and overlap the vinyl square. Sew the three rickrack lengths to pillow front. Sew loose ends of fourth rickrack length to pillow front (center portion will remain open to insert photo).

Step 3. Sew one daisy button at each corner of vinyl pocket.

Step 4. Position and pin white cord to pillow front as shown in Fig. 2.

Step 5. Place pillow front and back right sides together.

Sew around perimeter with ¼" seam allowance, leaving a 4" opening at lower edge. Turn right side out, stuff with polyester fiberfill and close opening with hand stitches.

Step 6. Insert 3" x 3" photo in vinyl pocket. ✄

Huggy Bears Backpack

By June Fiechter

Any little girl in your life will love this soft, totable backpack. And you will love how easy it is to make with scrap-basket materials you already have on hand.

Project Specifications

Skill Level: Beginner

Backpack Size: Approximately 13" x 15¾" x 2"

Materials

- Blue print fabric 14" x 36" for bag
- Bag lining fabric 14" x 36"
- Batting 14" x 36"
- Two 2" x 40" tan checked fabric strips for strap
- 2" x 40" batting for strap
- Tan checked fabric 7" x 8" for bear appliqué
- 7" x 8" batting for bear appliqué
- 1 yard cotton cord for drawstring
- 12" length of 2½"-wide soft pastel- shaded ribbon
- All-purpose thread to match fabrics
- Black, brown and pink machine-embroidery thread
- 4 (¹⁄₁₆") black beads for eyes
- Craft glue
- Basic sewing supplies and tools

Instructions

Step 1. On the right side of the blue print fabric mark ¾" buttonhole placement 1½" down from center top as shown in Fig. 1.

Step 2. On right side of blue print fabric mark one strap placement centered and 2" up from bottom edge, also shown in Fig. 1. Second and third strap placement marks should be 14" up from bottom edge and 3" from each side.

Step 3. Trace bear pattern on 7" x 8" tan checked fabric. Cut out

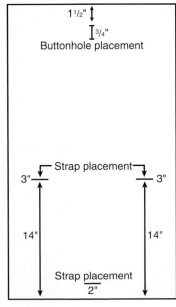

Fig. 1
Mark buttonhole and strap placement as shown.

on traced line. Use pattern to cut slightly smaller bear shape from 7" x 8" batting.

Step 4. Layer bear shape on batting shape; center on bag 5½" down from buttonhole mark. With brown machine-embroidery thread, machine-appliqué around all shapes as shown on pattern except face and lines in ears. Use black machine-embroidery thread to embroider face. Use pink machine-embroidery thread to embroider lines in ears and cheek areas.

Step 5. Place 14" x 36" batting between appliquéd bag fabric and lining. Machine-quilt ¼" around outside of bear shapes.

Step 6. Machine-quilt entire surface as desired.

Step 7. Place two 2" x 40" tan checked strips right sides together. Top with 2" x 40" batting strip. Sew two long edges with ¼" seam. Turn right side out. Turn short ends to inside and close with hand stitches.

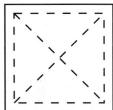

Fig. 2
Sew straps with X shape as shown.

Step 8. Find center of strap and place at lowest centered mark 2" from lower edge. Secure in place by sewing with X as shown in Fig. 2.

Step 9. Place two ends of strap on remaining two marks, ends pointing down toward bottom edge as shown in Fig. 3. Sew with X as shown.

Step 10. Bring top and bottom edges of bag together, right sides facing. Sew ½" side seams. To form box bottom of bag, pull side seams out to a point at each side. Sew a seam across each

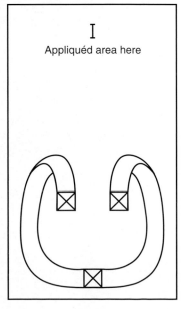

Fig. 3
Place and sew straps as shown.

side 1" from point as shown in Fig. 4.

Step 11. Work buttonhole where previously marked in Step 1. Turn under 1¼" at top of bag. Topstitch very close to top of bag and

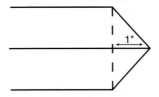

Fig. 4
Sew across points as shown to form box bottom.

again 1" from top of bag (just outside each end of but- tonhole). Turn bag right side out. Run cotton cord through casing formed. Tie a knot in each end of cord.

Step 12. Glue two black beads to each bear for eyes. Tie the 2½"-wide pink-and-blue ribbon in a bow. Stitch or glue to top of left bear's head. ✄

**Huggy Bears Backpack
Bear Pattern**

Noah's Friends
Play Pad & Finger Puppets

By Connie Matricardi

Cuddle up with your little one and enjoy an interactive story with an arkload of animal friends.

Project Specifications

Skill Level: Beginner

Blanket Size: Approximately 30" x 36"

Materials

- Light blue recycled blanket remnant or fleece fabric 30" x 36"
- ⅓ yard or 12" x 36" piece of gray felt
- Felt scraps of gold, white, royal blue, light blue, pink, green, red, tan, black, brown and orange
- 4 yards extra-wide double-fold blue bias tape to match blanket
- 20" piece of extra-wide double-fold gray bias tape to match gray felt
- 1 package royal blue medium rickrack
- Black and white paint markers
- Fabric glue
- 2 (5mm) black pompoms
- 3½" red chenille stem
- All-purpose threads to match fabrics
- Basic sewing supplies and tools

Instructions

Step 1. Round the corners of the 30" x 36" blanket.

Step 2. Trace and cut all pieces as directed on patterns. From gray felt cut one rectangle 5½" x 11" for the house portion of the ark.

Step 3. Bind straight upper edge of boat portion of ark with gray extra-wide double-fold bias tape. Referring to photo, arrange portholes on boat and sew in place. Pin royal blue rickrack on boat as indicated on pattern. After rickrack is in place, trim felt to follow line of rickrack.

Step 4. Referring to photo, pin boat, house, flags and roof to blanket. Pin a wavy line of rickrack to blanket on each side of boat, extending ½" under boat. Sew rickrack in place.

Step 5. Sew pieces in place, overlapping where necessary. Do not sew across the top of boat. Leave open to insert finger puppets. Sew a straight line across boat just above and below portholes.

Step 6. Pin sun, clouds, bird, leaves, fish and octopus to blanket, referring to photo for placement. Overlap pieces where necessary and sew to blanket. Sew leaves in place as shown in Fig. 1.

Fig. 1
Sew leaves in place as shown.

Step 7. With black paint draw eye on goldfish and two eyes and smile on octopus and sun. Use white paint to draw eye on royal blue fish and bird.

Step 8. Bind blanket with extra-wide double-fold blue bias tape.

Step 9. To make monkey finger puppet, glue ear shape to body back. Place body front and back together and sew around edges, leaving bottom open. Glue face shape to body front. Use black paint to mark eyes, nose and mouth. Glue red chenille stem to body back and bend as shown in Fig. 2.

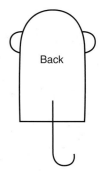

Back

Fig. 2
Glue and bend monkey tail as shown.

Step 10. Sew pig body front to body back, leaving open at bottom. Glue pig head front to body front, overlapping ½". Glue pig head back to body back. Glue pig nose to face. Glue two black pompoms to nose. Use black paint to mark eyes and mouth.

Step 11. Sew giraffe body front to body back, leaving open at bottom. Glue giraffe head front to body front, overlapping ½". Glue giraffe head back to body back. Glue spots to body and ear shapes to ears. Use black paint to mark eyes and nostrils.

Step 12. Glue hippo arm shape to body back. Sew hippo body front to body back, leaving open at bottom.

Glue hippo teeth to underside of head front. Glue head to body same as pig and giraffe. Use black paint to mark eyes and nostrils.

Step 13. Sew lion body front to body back, leaving open at bottom. Glue lion mane to body front, overlapping ¾". Glue second mane to body back. Glue lion face to mane. Glue nose on face. Use black paint to mark eyes and whiskers. ✄

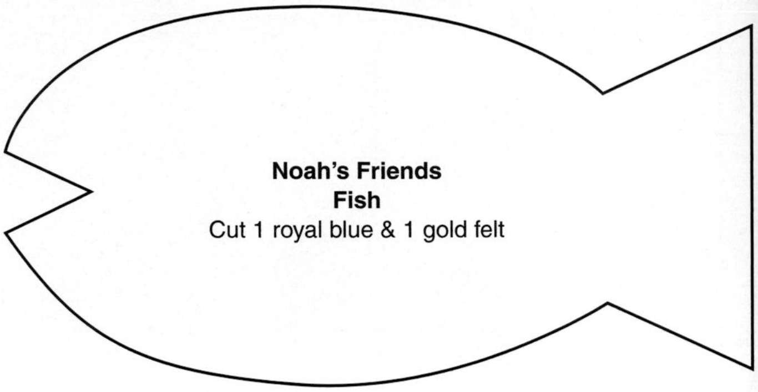

**Noah's Friends
Fish**
Cut 1 royal blue & 1 gold felt

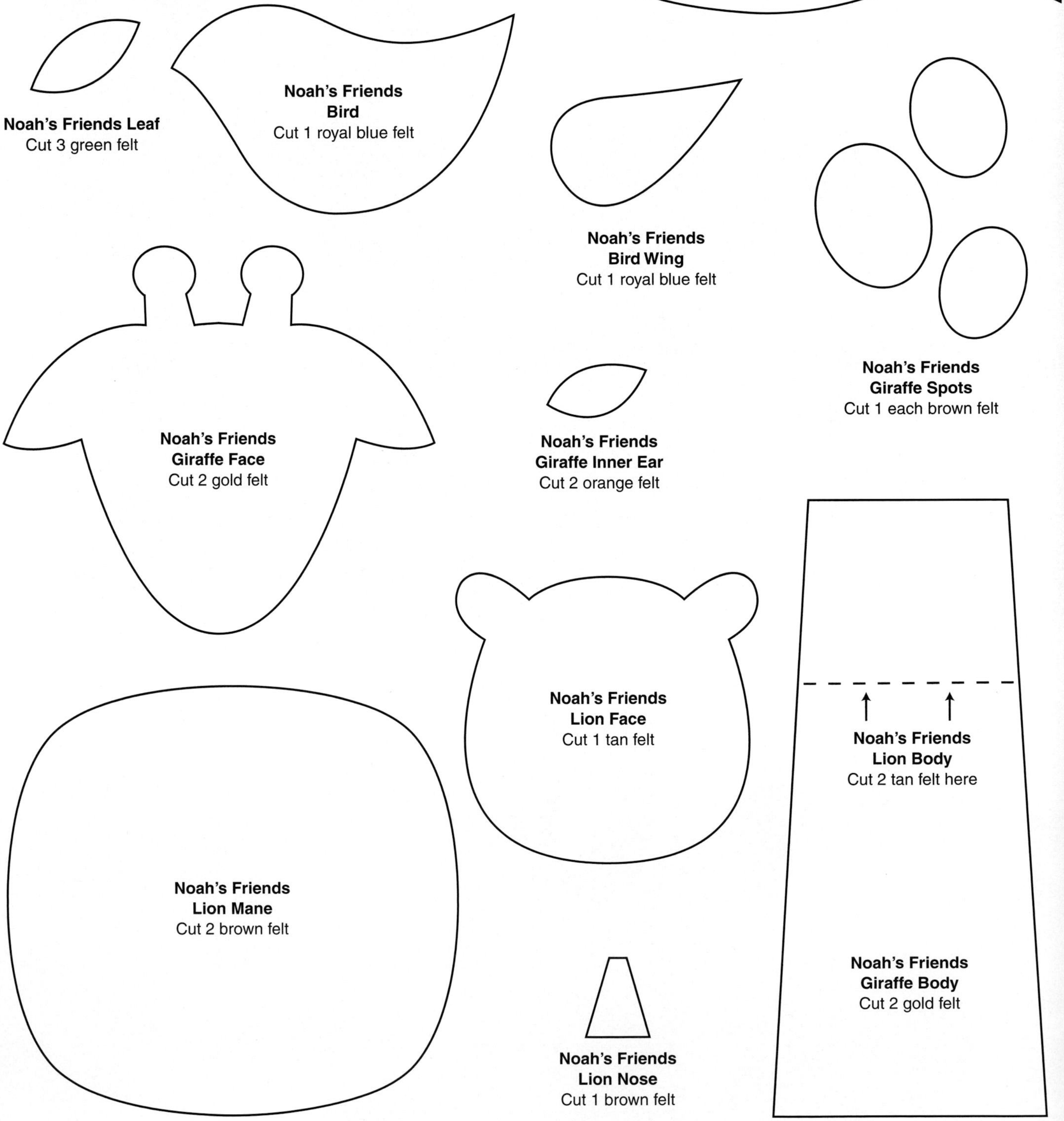

Noah's Friends Leaf
Cut 3 green felt

**Noah's Friends
Bird**
Cut 1 royal blue felt

**Noah's Friends
Bird Wing**
Cut 1 royal blue felt

**Noah's Friends
Giraffe Spots**
Cut 1 each brown felt

**Noah's Friends
Giraffe Face**
Cut 2 gold felt

**Noah's Friends
Giraffe Inner Ear**
Cut 2 orange felt

**Noah's Friends
Lion Face**
Cut 1 tan felt

**Noah's Friends
Lion Body**
Cut 2 tan felt here

**Noah's Friends
Lion Mane**
Cut 2 brown felt

**Noah's Friends
Giraffe Body**
Cut 2 gold felt

**Noah's Friends
Lion Nose**
Cut 1 brown felt

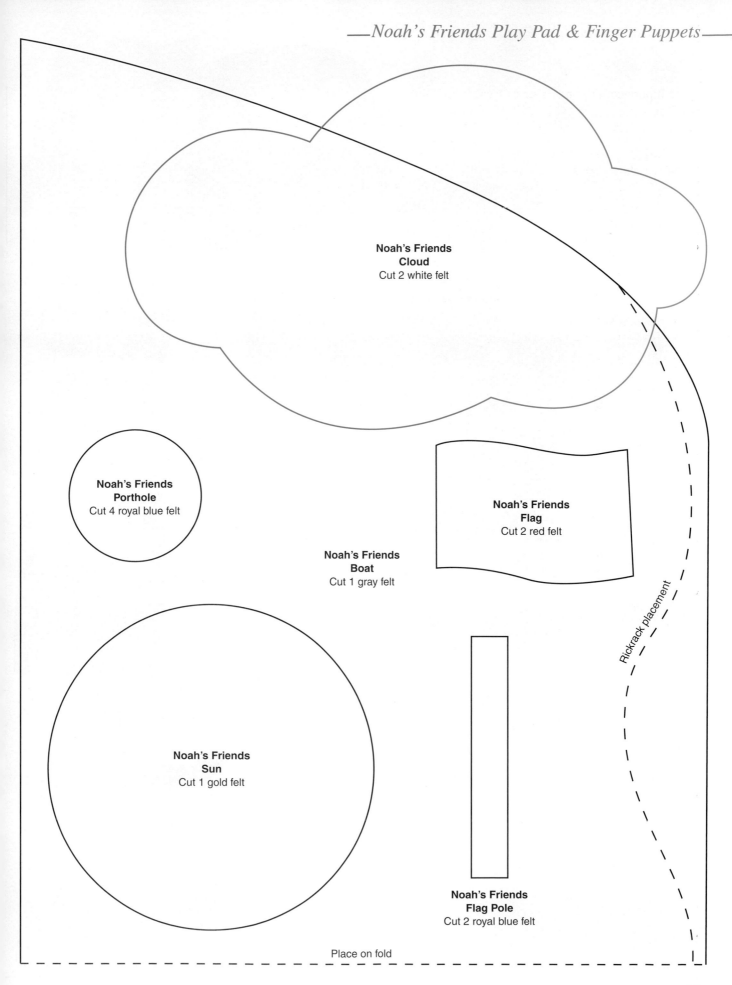

**Noah's Friends
Cloud**
Cut 2 white felt

**Noah's Friends
Porthole**
Cut 4 royal blue felt

**Noah's Friends
Boat**
Cut 1 gray felt

**Noah's Friends
Flag**
Cut 2 red felt

Rickrack placement

**Noah's Friends
Sun**
Cut 1 gold felt

**Noah's Friends
Flag Pole**
Cut 2 royal blue felt

Place on fold

Place on fold

**Noah's Friends
Ark Roof**
Cut 1 gray felt

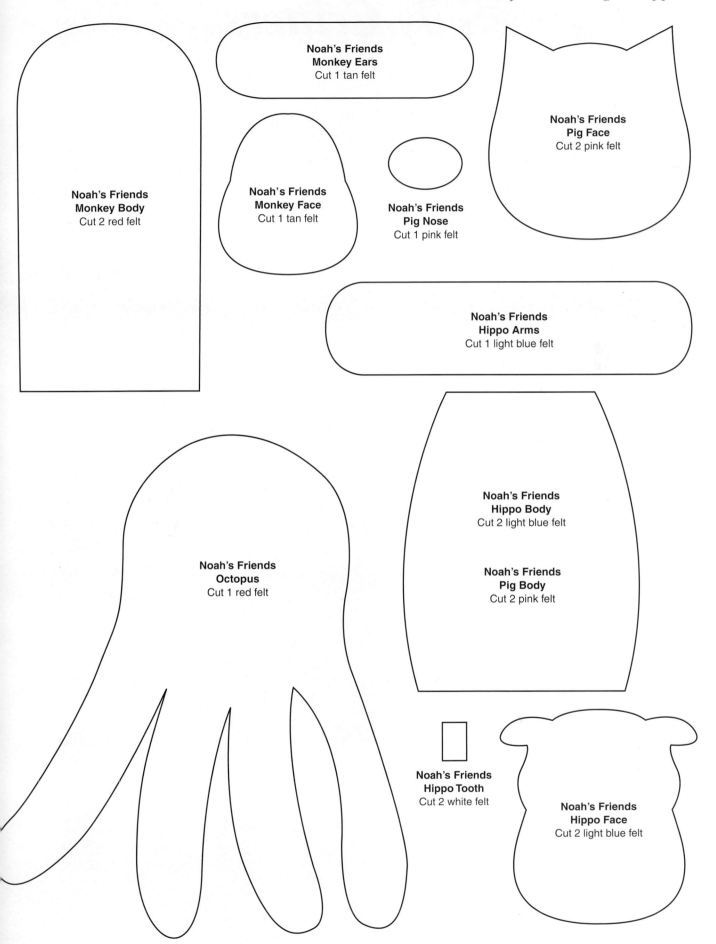

Noah's Friends
Monkey Ears
Cut 1 tan felt

Noah's Friends
Pig Face
Cut 2 pink felt

Noah's Friends
Monkey Body
Cut 2 red felt

Noah's Friends
Monkey Face
Cut 1 tan felt

Noah's Friends
Pig Nose
Cut 1 pink felt

Noah's Friends
Hippo Arms
Cut 1 light blue felt

Noah's Friends
Octopus
Cut 1 red felt

Noah's Friends
Hippo Body
Cut 2 light blue felt

Noah's Friends
Pig Body
Cut 2 pink felt

Noah's Friends
Hippo Tooth
Cut 2 white felt

Noah's Friends
Hippo Face
Cut 2 light blue felt

Silly Critters

By Diana Stunell-Dunsmore

Children love to celebrate holidays! From fabric scraps and trims, make these cute bows to be worn as pins or barrettes to make special occasions festive.

Project Specifications

Skill Level: Beginner

Pin/barrette Size: Approximately 4" x 2½"

Materials

For Birthday Bear

- 2 rectangles novelty birthday print 3" x 4½" for bow tie
- 1 rectangle coordinating solid fabric 3" x 4¼" for body, plus scraps for ears
- 5½" (⅛"-wide) contrasting satin ribbon
- 2 black seed beads for eyes
- 1 (5mm) black bead or pompom
- Black 6-strand embroidery floss

For Christmas Mouse

- 2 rectangles red Christmas print 3" x 4½" for bow tie
- 1 rectangle solid white fabric 3" x 4¼" for body, plus scraps for ears
- 5½" (⅛"-wide) red satin ribbon
- 2 black seed beads for eyes
- 2 white seed beads for teeth
- 1 (5mm) pink pompom
- Black 6-strand embroidery floss

For Easter Bunny

- 2 rectangles solid pink fabric 3" x 4½" for bow tie
- 1 rectangle pink-and-white print fabric 3" x 4¼" for body, plus scraps for ears
- 5½" (⅛"-wide) pink satin ribbon
- 2 green seed beads for eyes
- 1 (5mm) pink pompom
- Pink 6-strand embroidery floss

For Halloween Cat

- 2 rectangles novelty Halloween print 3" x 4½" for bow tie
- 1 rectangle solid black fabric 3" x 4¼" for body, plus scraps for ears
- 5½" (⅛"-wide) yellow satin ribbon

- 2 yellow seed beads for eyes
- 1 (5mm) orange bead or pompom
- 1 (5mm) jingle bell
- Gold 6-strand embroidery floss

For Each Pin/Barrette

- 2 rectangles medium-weight interfacing 3" x 4½" (regular or fusible)
- Small amount of polyester fiberfill
- Safety pin (2") or barrette (3⅜")
- All-purpose thread to match fabrics
- Basic sewing supplies and tools

Instructions

Step 1. For each silly critter baste or fuse two interfacing pieces to two 3" x 4½" bow tie pieces. Right sides facing, sew bow tie pieces together, leaving an opening for turning. Clip corners, turn right side out and close opening with hand stitches. Press and run a line of gathering stitches across the short center of the piece. Pull up stitches to 1½" to create bow shape.

Step 2. Fold the appropriate 3" x 4¼" fabric piece lengthwise, right sides together. Sew long edge and turn right side out for head/body. Press with center seam at back.

Step 3. Stitch line across head/body strip, dividing head and body, as shown in Fig. 1. Stuff very lightly above and below line with polyester fiberfill to create head and body.

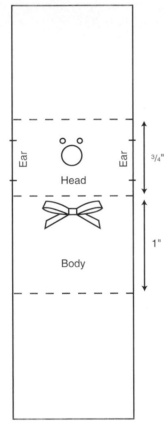

Fig. 1
Stitch lines across head/body strip as shown.

Stitch another line ¾" above first line, enclosing fiberfill and creating head area. Stitch another line 1" below first line, enclosing fiberfill and creating body area. Zigzag across both open ends of strip.

Step 4. Referring to Fig. 2, add appropriate facial details for each silly critter. Refer to Fig. 3 for stitch instructions. Make stitches through all layers for quilted appearance.

Birthday Bear: Use 1 strand of black embroidery floss to straight-stitch mouth. Sew on black 5mm bead for nose and two black seed beads for eyes.

Christmas Mouse: Use 1 strand of black embroidery floss to straight-stitch mouth and whiskers. Sew on pink 5mm pompom for nose and two black seed beads for eyes. Sew two white seed beads in place for teeth.

Easter Bunny: Use 1 strand of pink embroidery floss to backstitch mouth and straight-stitch whiskers. Sew on pink 5mm pompom for nose and two green seed beads for eyes.

Backstitch   Straight Stitch

Fig. 3

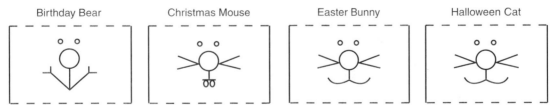

Birthday Bear   Christmas Mouse   Easter Bunny   Halloween Cat

Fig. 2
Add facial details for each critter as shown.

Halloween Cat: Use 1 strand of gold embroidery floss to backstitch mouth and straight-stitch whiskers. Sew on orange 5mm pompom or bead for nose and two yellow seed beads for eyes.

Step 5. Trace and cut ears as directed on pattern for each silly critter. Place two matching ear pieces right sides together, leaving straight edge open. Trim seam, clip curves and turn right side out. Stuff very lightly with polyester fiberfill. Gather straight edge through both thicknesses. Pull up tightly and knot. Repeat for second ear. Pin ears to back of head area with approximately ⅜" seam allowance. Hand-stitch in place.

Step 6. Tie appropriate 5½" piece of ⅛"-wide ribbon in a bow. Trim ends diagonally. Sew in place on body as shown in photo. Sew 5mm jingle bell to cat's bow.

Step 7. For mouse tail cut two 4" lengths of white embroidery floss. Knot ends together and thread through bottom center of body, back to front. Divide floss into three sets of four strands each and braid. Knot close to end and trim.

Step 8. For cat tail cut six 4½" lengths of black embroidery floss. Divide into three sets of two lengths. Knot ends of each set of two lengths together and thread each separately through bottom center of body, back to front. Braid the three sets. Knot close to end and trim.

Step 9. Center animal head/body strip on bow tie and bring zigzagged ends to center back. Hand-stitch ends together. Tack sides of strip to bow tie back at animal's neckline, going through bow tie and catching underside of animal strip. Knot at back of bow tie.

Step 10. Open safety pin or barrette. Slide through bottom half of center strip. Tack pin or barrette in place through center strip. Also tack safety pin spring end to back layer of bow tie as shown in Fig. 4. ✄

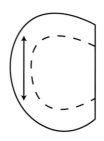

**Silly Critters
Bear Ear**
Cut 4 coordinating solid

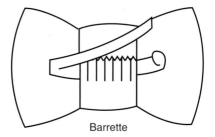

Barrette

Safety Pin

Fig. 4
Insert safety pin or barrette as shown.

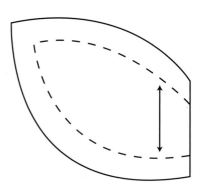

**Silly Critters
Bunny Ear**
Cut 4 pink-and-white print

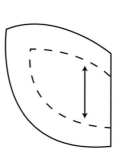

**Silly Critters
Cat Ear**
Cut 4 black

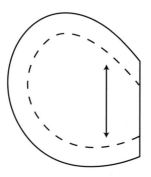

**Silly Critters
Mouse Ear**
Cut 4 white

Roly-Poly Lamb

By Diana Stunell-Dunsmore

This cuddly little lamb is constructed entirely of circles and sewn by hand.
A great group project—few supplies are needed and only basic sewing skills.

Project Specifications

Skill Level: Beginner

Lamb Size: Approximately 17" circumference

Materials

- ⅓ yard white fleece
- ¼ yard black T-shirt knit
- 1 (⅝") bell
- Scrap of ⅛"-wide pink ribbon
- 2 (3mm or 4mm) white beads or 6-strand white embroidery floss
- 3 strands of light pink embroidery floss
- Black and white all-purpose sewing thread
- Polyester fiberfill
- Sturdy sewing needle
- Needle-nose pliers
- Basic sewing supplies and tools

Instructions

Step 1. Trace and cut pieces as directed on patterns.

Step 2. Using doubled white thread, run a gathering stitch close to the edge around the circumference of the lamb body. Place a very large handful of polyester fiberfill in the center of the body circle and pull up the thread as tightly as possible; securely knot. The circle will not be closed because of the thickness of the fabric. Add more fiberfill if necessary to fill out body shape.

Step 3. Using doubled black thread, run a gathering stitch close to the edge around the circumference of the lamb head. Place a small amount of polyester fiberfill in the center of the head circle and pull up the thread as tightly as possible; securely knot. Take two long vertical stitches on the back of the head and pull top and bottom of head together to give head a more oval shape.

Step 4. Using doubled black thread, run a gathering stitch close to the edge around the circumference of each ear. Pull up the thread as tightly as possible; securely knot. The ears are not stuffed. Attach ears to back of head with hand stitches.

Fig. 1
Place eyes on face as shown.

Step 5. Referring to Fig. 1, with white thread sew white beads to front of head for eyes. Insert needle from back of head and return to back of head to knot. ***Designer Note:*** *To baby-proof, use white embroidery floss and make French knots with two wraps around the needle.*

Step 6. With 3 strands of light pink embroidery floss, embroider nose and mouth. Referring to Fig. 2, bring needle up at A, down at B, leaving floss loose enough to form nose. Come up at C and bring floss over the A-B strands, pulling tightly enough to form a V. Go down at D. Come up again very near D and form a triple-wrapped French knot.

Fig. 2
Embroider face as shown.

Step 7. Thread the scrap of pink ribbon through bell loop. Fold ribbon in half and tack ends together on back of face.

Step 8. With doubled white thread, position and sew head securely to body over fleece opening. Use

needle-nose pliers to help pull the needle through the thick layers. Sew all around head two or three times. Leave bell and ears free.

Step 9. Using doubled black thread, run a gathering stitch close to the edge around the circumference of one lamb foot. Place a very small amount of polyester fiberfill in the center of the foot circle and pull up the thread as tightly as possible; securely knot. Repeat for four feet.

Step 10. Pin feet to bottom of body. Position with all four feet touching each other. With doubled black thread, sew each foot to body as shown in Fig. 3.

Step 11. Using doubled white thread, run a gathering stitch close to the edge around the circumference of lamb tail. Place a tiny amount of polyester fiberfill in the center of the tail circle and pull up the thread as tightly as possible; securely knot, but do not cut thread. Sew tail securely to lamb's backside. ✂

Fig. 3
Position feet on bottom of body as shown.

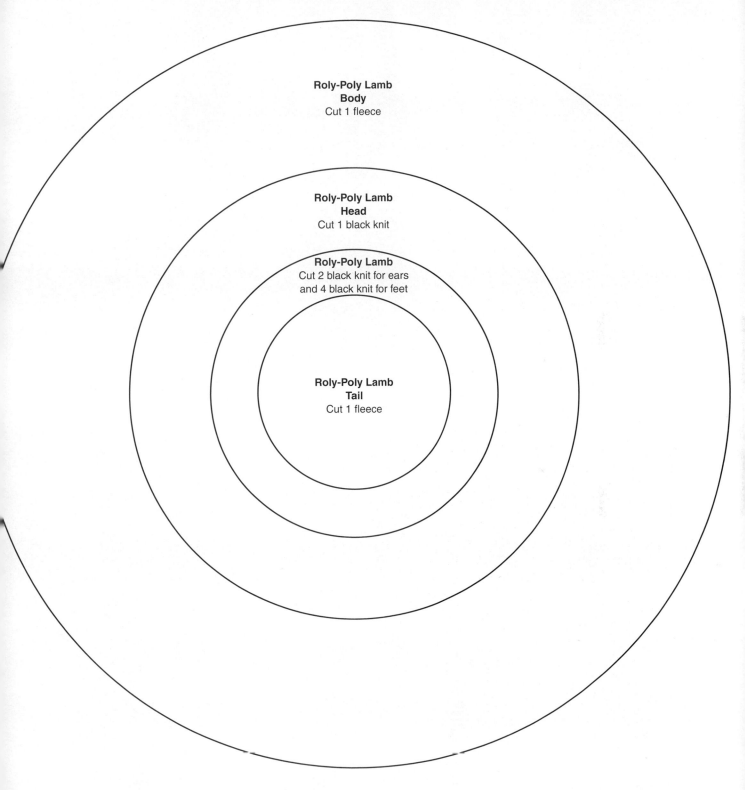

**Roly-Poly Lamb
Body**
Cut 1 fleece

**Roly-Poly Lamb
Head**
Cut 1 black knit

Roly-Poly Lamb
Cut 2 black knit for ears
and 4 black knit for feet

**Roly-Poly Lamb
Tail**
Cut 1 fleece

(Enlarge all patterns 154% before cutting)

The Sewing Room

Just imagine—your very own sewing room full of everything you need and want to make sewing your favorite pastime. And what more appropriate place to have projects using fabric scraps!

Our Sew Happy wall hanging is a real pleaser with lots of pockets to keep scissors, thread, thimbles and many other small items better organized.

And be sure to check out the I'm So Cool Frog Pincushion. He'll keep your pins all in one place and give you a smile each time you see him lounging on your sewing table!

You'll want to get started on one of these projects right away!

Sewing Basket

By Pearl Louise Krush

Although considered a sewing room accessory, the very nature of this attractive basket will make it most useful to you when carried room to room.

Project Specifications

Skill Level: Beginner

Sewing Basket Size: Any size

Materials

- Small basket with handle
- Thin cardboard for basket top and bottom
- 1 yard of fabric
- 2 coordinating fabric strips 1½" x 25"
- Scraps of thin batting
- Small pincushion (optional)
- Cool-temperature glue gun and glue
- Pattern paper
- Basic sewing supplies and tools

Instructions

Step 1. Measure depth of basket sides. Double that measurement and add 1". Cut a strip across fabric by

that measurement. (For example: If your basket is 3" deep, cut 7" strip across fabric width.)

Step 2. Fold fabric strip lengthwise, wrong sides together; press. Finger-fold and pin 1" pleats on the raw edges of the folded strip. Sew in place.

Step 3. Place pleated fabric strip in basket. Measure to fit so that ends overlap. Sew overlapped ends together. Place strip in basket, pushing raw edges into basket bottom.

Step 4. Trace around basket bottom on pattern paper. Cut out for pattern. Cut a piece of thin cardboard and a thin batting piece this size. Cut a piece of fabric 1" larger than pattern piece.

Step 5. Layer batting between thin cardboard and fabric. Turn layers over onto work surface. Run a bead of glue around outer edge of cardboard shape. Pull fabric edge over onto glue. Glue layered piece into bottom of basket.

Step 6. Glue pleated edge of fabric lining to top edge of basket.

Step 7. Cut a paper pattern to fit basket top. Cut slight indentations at sides to accommodate basket handles. Use pattern to cut two thin cardboard pieces and one thin batting piece. Cut two pieces of fabric ½" larger than pattern. Clip curved edges of fabric all around.

Step 8. For basket lid, layer batting between one thin cardboard piece and one fabric piece. Turn layers over onto work surface. Run a bead of glue around outer edge of cardboard shape. Pull fabric edge over onto glue.

Step 9. Repeat Step 8 with fabric and thin cardboard only for lid lining. Glue lining to reverse side of basket lid, glued edges facing.

Step 10. Bend lid slightly at center and place on basket.

Step 11. Fold long edges of one coordinting fabric strip to center, wrong sides facing; press. Fold lengthwise again, bringing folded edges together. Fold short ends in and topstitch. Repeat with second coordinating fabric strip. Sew or glue to sides of basket lid and tie around handles.

Designer Note: A small pincushion can be tied or glued to basket handle if desired. ✂

Thread Organizer

By Pearl Louise Krush

Spend a little time organizing your threads and your sewing room.
You'll benefit by having more time to create with such functional accessories.

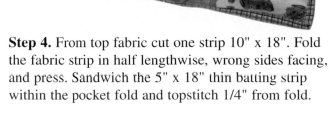

Project Specifications

Skill Level: Beginner

Thread Organizer Size: Approximately 16½" x 22"

Materials

- 1½ yards of fabric for top
- ¾ yard coordinating fabric for backing and binding
- Cardboard 16½" x 22"
- Thin batting 17½" x 23" and 5" x 18"
- 1½ yards ¼"-wide elastic
- Sturdy plastic coat hanger
- Box of 1" brass safety pins
- Small pincushion (optional)
- All-purpose threads to match fabrics
- Basic sewing supplies and tools

Instructions

Step 1. Round top corners of cardboard to match curve of coat hanger as shown in Fig. 1.

Step 2. Using cardboard as a pattern, cut one piece each from top fabric, backing fabric and thin batting, adding ½" on all sides

Step 3. Fold the backing fabric in half lengthwise and press to mark center back. Make a ¼" slit in the top center of backing fabric 2" from the top edge for later insertion of coat hanger.

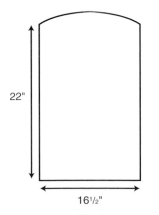

22"

16½"

Fig. 1
Round top corners of
cardboard as shown.

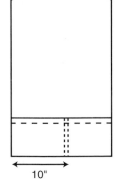

10"

Fig. 2
Attach pocket with double
vertical seams as shown.

Step 4. From top fabric cut one strip 10" x 18". Fold the fabric strip in half lengthwise, wrong sides facing, and press. Sandwich the 5" x 18" thin batting strip within the pocket fold and topstitch 1/4" from fold.

Step 5. Place thin batting cut in Step 2 on work surface. Place top fabric piece on batting, right side up. Align long raw edges of pocket with lower edge of top/batting layers. Sew a vertical double seam 10" from left side to attach pocket as shown in Fig. 2.

Step 6. From top fabric cut four 4" strips across the

width of the fabric. Fold each strip in half lengthwise, right sides facing, and stitch a ¼" seam along the aligned long raw edges. Repeat for four strips. Turn each right side out; press. Topstitch each strip ½" from each long edge to form a casing through the center.

Step 7. Cut three 18" strips of ¼"-wide elastic. Pin a safety pin into the end of one elastic piece and thread through casing of one strip. Pin elastic at each end of strip to hold securely in place. Repeat for three strips.

Step 8. Position and pin each elastic/fabric strip on layered top and batting as shown in Fig. 3.

Step 9. Place backing piece on work surface, right side facing down. Place layered

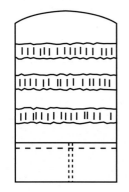

Fig. 3
Position elastic/fabric strips on organizer as shown.

top and batting on backing. Stitch around edges of layers, leaving bottom edge open.

Step 10. From backing fabric cut and join enough 2½" fabric strips to make 2½ yards of binding. Fold lengthwise, wrong sides together; press. Align raw edges of binding with outer edges of layered thread organizer and sew around perimeter, sewing only to top layer and batting at lower edge.

Step 11. Starting at one lower edge, bring folded edge of binding to back and sew in place with hand stitches around side and top edges. Stop at the other lower edge. Insert hanger into thread organizer and bring hook out through slit cut in Step 3. Insert cardboard between batting and backing. Continue to sew binding to back of thread organizer, closing lower opening.

Step 12. Place thread spools in elastic strips and pin brass safety pins between each spool to hold in place. Store scissors and rotary cutter in pocket. Tie small pincushion to hanger if desired. ✄

Sew Happy Sampler

By Chris Malone

Make and hang a cheery wall quilt in your sewing room to lift your spirits and brighten your work space. Little pockets are handy for stashing your supplies!

Project Specifications

Skill Level: Beginner

Wall Quilt Size: 11" x 25"

Materials

- ¼ yard red-and-tan print for borders and pocket lining
- 7½" x 7½" square and 2 strips 4½" x 8½" tan with red print
- 7" x 7" tan solid square
- Assorted red, blue, gold, green, cream and tan scraps
- Backing 15" x 29"
- Thin batting 15" x 29"
- 7 (¾"–1") red and tan buttons
- Embroidery hoop and needle
- Red 6-strand embroidery floss
- All-purpose threads to match fabrics
- 1 spool red hand-quilting thread
- 1⅝" x 18" wooden ruler
- Spray varnish for ruler, if needed
- Freezer paper
- Air- or water-soluble marker
- No-fray product
- 2 small picture hangers
- Rotary-cutting tools
- Basic sewing supplies and tools

Instructions

Log Cabin Block

Step 1. From red scrap cut center square 1½" x 1½". Cut 1½" strips from six different tan scraps. Cut 1½" strips from six different colored scraps.

Step 2. Sew a tan strip to red center square. Trim even with red square; press. Continue to add tan and colored strips Log Cabin style as shown in Fig. 1. Trim each piece even with square and press seam toward center. Add 12 strips until block measures 7½" x 7½".

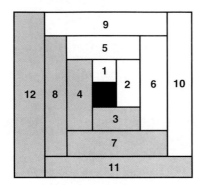

Fig. 1
Sew tan and colored strips around
center square in order shown.

Appliquéd Heart Block

Step 1. Trace heart and words on tan solid fabric with air- or water-soluble marker. Trace heart outline on paper side of freezer paper.

Step 2. Place marked fabric in embroidery hoop. With 2 strands of red embroidery floss, backstitch the letters. Cut out heart approximately ¼" outside traced outline.

Step 3. Remove marked lines with a spritz of water or immerse piece in cool water. Allow to dry thoroughly.

Step 4. Place heart face down on work surface. Center freezer-paper heart face down on fabric heart; press to adhere. Turn and press fabric seam allowance over to the back of the freezer paper. Clip curved edges. Press well and remove freezer paper. If desired, baste around folded edge of heart.

Step 5. Center heart right side up on 7½" x 7½" tan with red print square. Pin in place. With 3 strands of red embroidery floss, work buttonhole stitch around heart.

Four-Patch Block

Step 1. From assorted colored scraps cut three squares 4" x 4" and four squares 2¼" x 2¼".

Step 2. Sew two 2¼" squares together and press seam allowance to one side. Sew the other two 2¼" squares together and press seam allowance in opposite direction. Sew two sets of squares together as shown in Fig. 2.

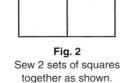

Fig. 2
Sew 2 sets of squares
together as shown.

Step 3. Sew 4" squares together with pieced Four-Patch as shown in Fig. 3.

Step 4. Apply no-fray product to top edge only of

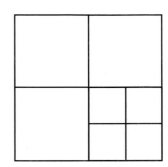

Fig. 3
Sew squares together as shown.

block. When dry, fold edge under ¼" and press. With 3 strands of red embroidery floss, work buttonhole stitch across top of block to secure hem.

Assembly

Step 1. Sew bottom of Log Cabin block to top of Heart block.

Step 2. From red-and-tan print cut a square 7½" x 7½". Sew to bottom of Heart block. Press seam allowances downward.

Step 3. Place Four-Patch block right side up over red-and-tan square. Baste together along side and bottom edges.

Step 4. From red-and-tan print cut two strips each 2½" x 21½" and 2½" x 11½". Sew the longer strips to the long sides of the pieced panel and the shorter strips to the top and bottom; press seam allowances toward borders.

Step 5. Place thin batting on work surface and smooth. Place backing fabric right side up on top of batting. Place pieced panel right side down on backing. Pin through all layers to secure. Trim backing and batting even with top.

Step 6. Sew around perimeter leaving 5" opening at center bottom. Trim batting close to seam and trim corners. Turn right side out and close opening with hand stitches.

Step 7. Baste layers with thread or pins. Hand-quilt in the ditch as close to the seams as possible between border and pieced blocks and at the seams between blocks.

Step 8. To form storage pockets, quilt the vertical seam between the squares of the Four-Patch block and the horizontal seam above the small Four-Patch. This will form one long and one short pocket.

Step 9. Fold 4½" x 8½" tan-and-red print strips in half lengthwise, right sides together, for hanging loops.

**Sew Happy Sampler
Heart Appliqué Pattern**

Sew along all raw edges of each piece, leaving 2"
opening in one long side. Clip corners and turn right
side out. Press and close openings with hand stitches.

Step 10. Fold one loop over top of wall quilt 2" from
side and overlapping top edge 1½" front and back. Sew
one of the ¾"–1" red buttons on the loop front and
through all layers. Repeat on other side.

Step 11. Sew one button to center of Log Cabin block,
one to the cleft of the heart and three down the center
of the Four-Patch as shown in the photo.

Step 12. If wooden ruler is unfinished, spray with two
light coats of varnish and dry thoroughly. Attach a picture hanger to each end of ruler on backside. Slip
through loops to hang. ✂

Heart Pocket Scissors Keeper

By Mary Ayres

Both functional and very pretty, this accessory is a perfect gift for even your non-sewing friends. All scissors need a known place to be found.

Project Specifications

Skill Level: Beginner

Scissors Pocket Size: Approximately 5⅛" x 9¼"

Materials

- Scraps of off-white faille, taffeta or other shiny fabric
- Scraps of unbleached muslin for backing
- Off-white doily scrap 6" x 7"
- Thin batting 6" x 10"
- 1 yard off-white piping
- 6" length of off-white ¼"-wide satin ribbon
- Basic sewing supplies and tools

Instructions

Step 1. Cut fabrics, batting and lace as directed on pattern.

Step 2. Place lace half heart on top of shiny half heart. Align raw edges of off-white piping with straight raw edges of lace/shiny half heart. Sew with ¼" seam. Place muslin half heart on top of all layers, aligning straight edges. Sew on previous sewing line. Turn right side out, with shiny fabric layered between lace and muslin.

Step 3. Baste wrong side of whole heart to batting. Place muslin side of assembled half heart facing fabric side of whole heart. Starting at lower edge, sew piping around entire perimeter, ending and overlapping at lower edge. Clip seam at cleft of heart as you sew, for a smooth turn.

Step 4. Align raw ends of off-white ¼" ribbon with raw edges of top of heart, each end 1" from heart cleft. Baste in place.

Step 5. Place whole muslin heart on top of all layers. Sew around perimeter, leaving 3" opening for turning.

Step 6. Clip cleft and rounded edges of heart. Turn right side out. Close opening with hand stitches. ✄

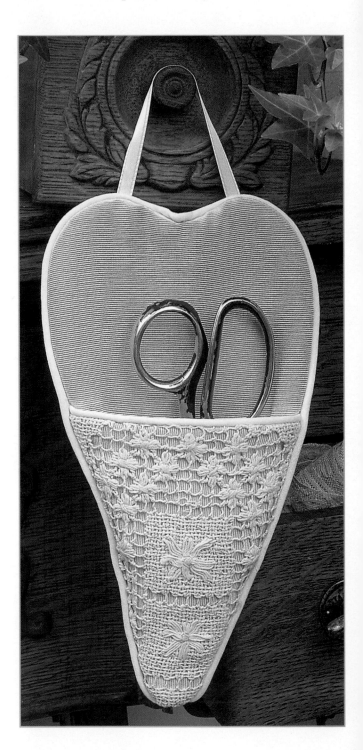

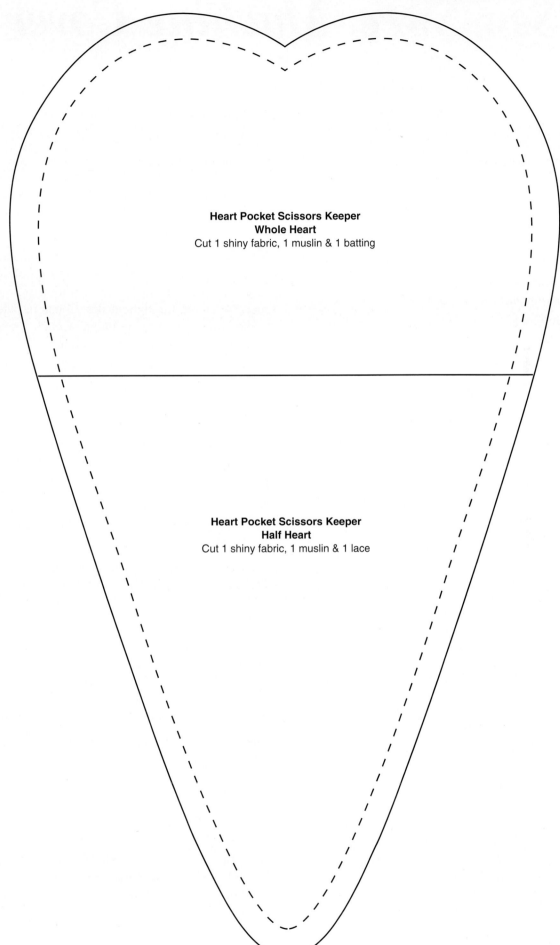

Heart Pocket Scissors Keeper
Whole Heart
Cut 1 shiny fabric, 1 muslin & 1 batting

Heart Pocket Scissors Keeper
Half Heart
Cut 1 shiny fabric, 1 muslin & 1 lace

Sew Sweet Machine Cover

By Bev Shenefield

*Your sewing machine is an important part of your life—
almost a member of the family. Give it the attractive cover it deserves!*

Project Specifications

Skill Level: Beginner

Sewing Machine Cover Size: Approximately 17½" x 12½" x 8"

Materials

- 1 yard prequilted fabric
- 1 yard coordinating check or plaid
- Gray felt 9" x 12"
- White felt 9" x 12"
- 4 yards ¾"-wide ruffled white eyelet trim
- White crochet cotton
- Gray and white 6-strand embroidery floss
- 1 (¼") two-hole black button
- 6–8 assorted buttons in coordinating colors
- Fabric glue
- Craft glue
- Scraps of fusible transfer web
- Regular and large-eye embroidery needles
- White all-purpose sewing thread
- Basic sewing supplies and tools

Instructions

Step 1. Trace and cut ends for machine cover as directed on pattern. Cut one piece each 18" x 23½" from prequilted and coordinating check or plaid.

Step 2. Trace appliqué shapes on paper side of fusible transfer web. Cut out leaving roughly ¼" margin around traced lines. Following manufacturer's instructions, fuse to selected fabrics. Cut out on traced lines.

Step 3. Referring to photo for placement, arrange appliqués on one end of 18" x 23" prequilted piece, which will be the front portion of the machine cover. Fuse in place.

Step 4. With regular embroidery needle and 2 strands of white embroidery floss, work buttonhole stitch around pincushion and scissors handles. With 2 strands of gray embroidery floss work buttonhole stitch around thimble, spool and scissors blades.

Step 5. Referring to photo for placement, trace needle

and pins on machine cover front. With 2 strands of gray embroidery floss, embroider needle, lines on scissors blades, pins and line on thimble. To make French knots on thimble, wind 2 strands of gray floss around needle four times.

Step 6. With large-eye embroidery needle and white crochet cotton, add rows of thread to spool. Referring to photo, arrange white crochet cotton, as shown on machine cover, through needle. Couch in place with white all-purpose sewing thread. Couch strands of white crochet cotton on pincushion.

Step 7. With hand stitches, sew a strip of ¾"-wide white eyelet trim to lower edge of pincushion.

Step 8. Pin ¾"-wide white eyelet trim around the two prequilted curved ends of machine cover (not across bottom edge). Find center top of each curved end and centers of 23½" sides of prequilted cover. Pin ends in place and machine-sew.

Step 9. Find center top of each coordinating check or plaid lining for ends and center of each 23½" cover lining. Pin and sew as in Step 8.

Step 10. Place lining in cover, wrong sides together. Pin lower edges together. Starting at center back, pin ¾"-wide white eyelet trim around lower edge of machine cover.

Step 11. From coordinating check or plaid cut two border pieces each 5" x 18" and 5" x 8". Cut four 3½" pieces of ¾"-wide eyelet trim. Sew to each short end of longer strips, aligning at one end only. Sew shorter border pieces between longer border pieces, making a ring.

Step 12. Right sides together, pin border ring around bottom of cover, matching seams of cover and border. Be sure eyelet-trimmed ends are the ends sewn to the cover, not the untrimmed ends. Sew border strip to cover.

Step 13. Turn border to inside of cover. Turn raw edge under ¼" and stitch by hand over seam.

Step 14. Starting at center back of cover lining, pin ¾"-wide white eyelet trim around entire lower edge of machine cover. Machine-stitch in place.

Step 15. Position ¼" black button on scissors blades

and glue with craft glue. Referring to photo, glue other buttons in place.

Step 16. Fasten turned-under ends of pincushion eyelet trim in place with fabric glue.

Designer's Note: *Cover is sized for an open-arm machine used on a table. If machine is in cabinet, omit lower coordinating border and finish lower edge with eyelet trim. Size can also be altered by cutting cover section smaller so that coordinating border can still be added.* ✂

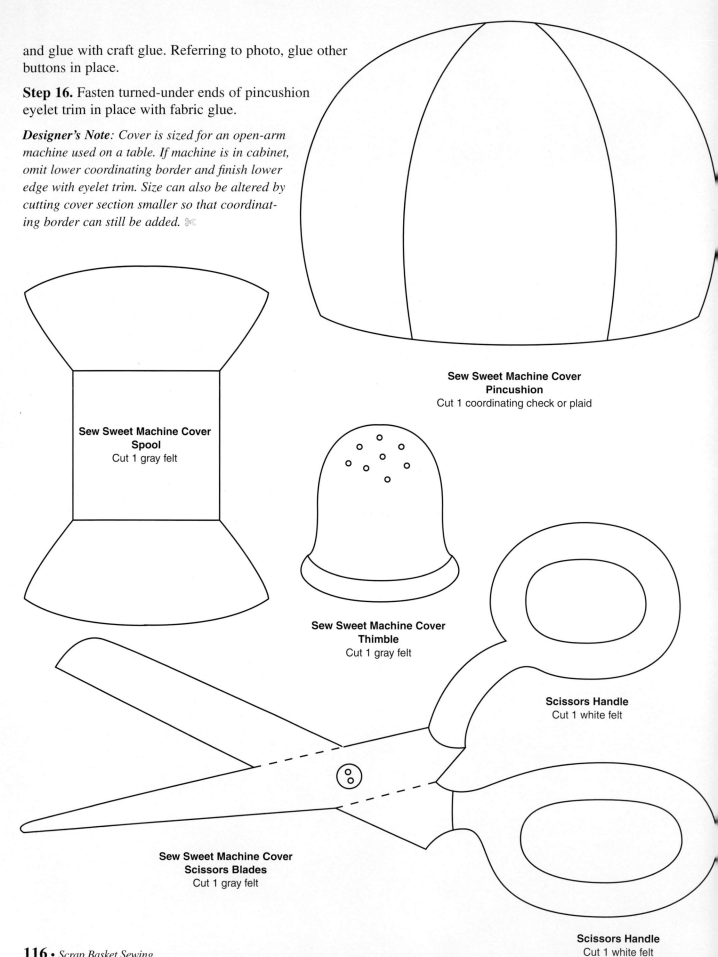

Sew Sweet Machine Cover Pincushion
Cut 1 coordinating check or plaid

Sew Sweet Machine Cover Spool
Cut 1 gray felt

Sew Sweet Machine Cover Thimble
Cut 1 gray felt

Scissors Handle
Cut 1 white felt

Sew Sweet Machine Cover Scissors Blades
Cut 1 gray felt

Scissors Handle
Cut 1 white felt

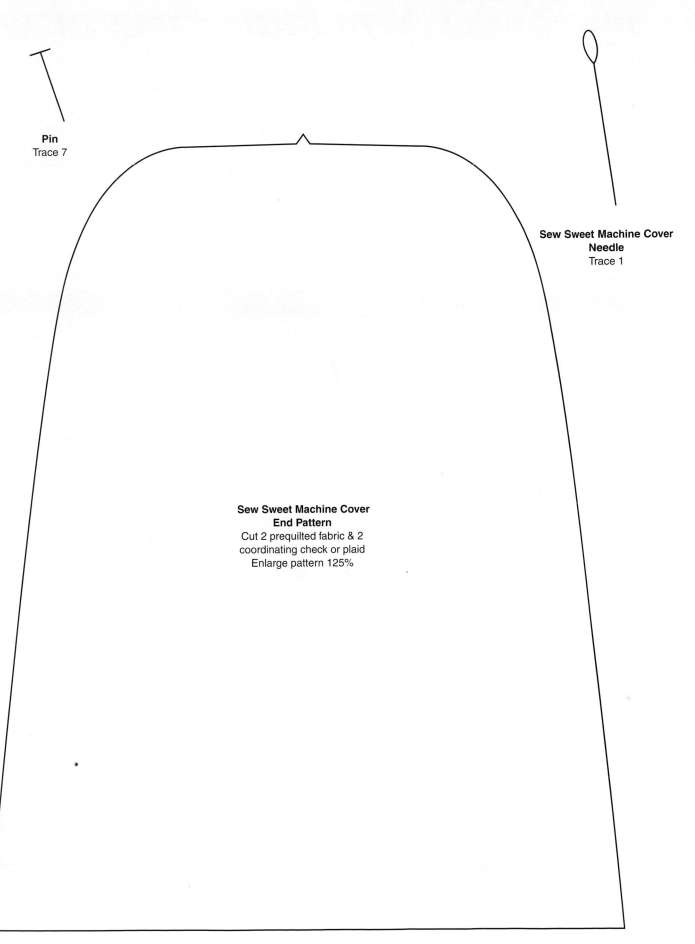

Pin
Trace 7

**Sew Sweet Machine Cover
Needle**
Trace 1

**Sew Sweet Machine Cover
End Pattern**
Cut 2 prequilted fabric & 2
coordinating check or plaid
Enlarge pattern 125%

Sew Sweet Armchair Organizer

By Bev Shenefield

No more fumbling for remote control, scissors, needles and pins! They will all be near at hand and ready when you use this handy sewing accessory.

Project Specifications

Skill Level: Beginner

Organizer Size: Approximately 7" x 19½"

Materials

- ½ yard prequilted fabric
- ½ yard coordinating check or plaid
- 3 yards ¾"-wide white ruffled eyelet trim
- White crochet cotton
- 3" plastic foam ball
- White all-purpose sewing thread
- Regular and large-eye embroidery needles
- Craft glue
- Fabric glue
- Recycled plastic bag
- 1 cup pellets or weighted material
- Basic sewing supplies and tools

Instructions

Step 1. Cut one piece each 7½" x 20" from prequilted and coordinating check or plaid fabric.

Step 2. For pockets cut one each 6½" x 9½", 7½" x 8½", 3¾" x 8½" and 5½" x 7½" from prequilted fabric. For pocket linings cut one each 7" x 9½", 7½" x 9", 4¼" x 8½" and 6" x 7½".

Step 3. Sew a 9½" piece of ¾"-wide white eyelet trim across one 9½" edge of 6½" x 9½" pocket. Place the 7" x 9½" piece of pocket lining over eyelet trim, right sides facing. Pin in place and machine-sew. Repeat with 7½" x 8½" pocket and 7½" x 9" lining, sewing across 7½" width. Repeat with 3¾" x 8½" pocket and 4¼" x 8½" lining, sewing across 8½" width. Repeat with 5½" x 7½" pocket and 6" x 7½" lining, sewing across 7½" width.

Step 4. Turn lining of each piece over to back, leaving about ¼" showing along top front of pocket.

Step 5. Place 6½" x 9½" pocket on 7½" x 8½" pocket, aligning side and bottom edges; pin. Find vertical center of each pocket and machine-stitch through all thicknesses top to bottom. Sew sides very close to edge. Sew across bottom, pleating extra fullness of top pocket along lower edge.

Step 6. Place 3¾" x 8½" pocket on 5½" x 7½" pocket, aligning side and bottom edges; pin. Beginning at top edge of 3¾" x 8½" pocket, stitch vertically top to bottom through all thicknesses to form two 2" pockets and one 3" pocket. Stitch very close to side edges. Pleat extra fullness of 3" pocket along lower edge and machine-stitch.

Step 7. Place one set of pockets right side up at each end of 7½" x 20" prequilted rectangle. Machine-sew through all layers very close to edge.

Step 8. Machine-stitch vertically down center of 5½" x 7½" pocket as far as possible and continue down length from back by hand.

Step 9. Starting at middle of end with three small pockets, pin ¾"-wide white eyelet trim along edge all the way around perimeter. Sew in place very close to edge.

Step 10. Place 7½" x 20" coordinating check or plaid rectangle on top of piece with pockets, right sides facing.

Step 11. Sew around perimeter, leaving 4" opening on one side for turning. Trim corners and turn right side out. Place pellets or weighted material inside organizer at end with small pockets. Machine-sew across organizer just above pockets. Weighted end will counterbalance weight of remote control, scissors, etc. on other end.

Step 12. Cut a 1" slice off 3" plastic foam ball. Cut one 7½" diameter circle from coordinating check or plaid fabric. Turn under edge of circle and gather edge. Place ball inside, flat side up, and pull gathers tightly. Adjust gathers evenly. Lace across opening with thread to pull fabric tighter on ball.

Step 13. Mark center of space between pockets. Place folded recycled plastic bag between quilted layer and lining area under center mark. Apply craft glue to bottom of pincushion ⅜" from edges. Center over mark and glue. Allow to dry thoroughly.

Step 14. Hand-sew lower fabric edge of pincushion to

organizer, being careful not so sew through lining. Place ¾"-wide white eyelet trim around edge of pincushion. Turn under end and glue in place with fabric glue. Allow to dry thoroughly.

Step 15. Close opening in side with hand stitches.

Step 16. Form six sections on pincushion by threading large-eye embroidery needle with white crochet cotton. Insert needle under eyelet trim and carry to opposite side of ball. Knot under eyelet trim. Repeat three times to make six sections. Couch with white all-purpose sewing thread. ✄

"I'm So Cool" Frog Pincushion

By June Fiechter

Being a pincushion is never easy, green or otherwise, but this good-natured frog will certainly add whimsy to the sewing room.

Project Specifications

Skill Level: Beginner

Pincushion Size: Approximately 8" x 18"

Materials

- 10" circle and 4" circle of medium green embossed felt for body and backing
- 2 strips 4½" x 10" medium green embossed felt for head/neck
- 2 pieces 2" x 4½" medium green embossed felt for eye areas
- 4 strips 4" x 13" medium green embossed felt for legs
- 4 strips 4" x 13" dark green embossed felt for legs
- 100" sturdy wire
- Roll of steel wool cut in half
- Black 6-strand embroidery floss
- Embroidery needle
- 70 (6mm) medium-green beads
- 20" piece of 1½"-wide soft green ribbon
- Polyester fiberfill
- Cosmetic blush and cotton swab
- Craft glue
- All-purpose threads to match felt
- 2 (⅝") craft eyes
- Basic sewing supplies and tools

Instructions

Note: Do not press embossed felt or it will lose its textured pattern.

Step 1. Trace and cut head/neck, legs and eye area as directed on patterns.

Step 2. Sew two rows of gathering stitches around the 10" body circle. Place the half roll of steel wool and a large handful of polyester fiberfill in the center of the body circle. Pull up the gathering threads to form body. Knot thread and apply craft glue to hold gathers in place.

Step 3. Place a medium green and a dark green embossed felt leg piece right sides together. Sew around perimeter, close to edge, leaving end open. Repeat for four legs. Turn right side out and topstitch close to sewn edges.

Step 4. Make an accordion pleat at each ankle as shown in Fig. 1. Stitch to secure.

Step 5. Cut sturdy wire into five 20" pieces. Bend each in a U-shape. Position one U-shaped wire in each leg. Stuff each leg with polyester fiberfill.

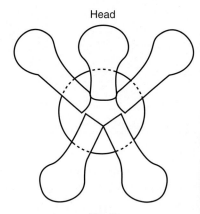

Fig. 1
Make an accordion pleat at each ankle as shown.

Step 6. Place two eye-area pieces right sides together. Stitch around perimeter, leaving open on the flat edge. Turn right side out and stuff with polyester fiberfill.

Step 7. Take one head/neck piece and measure in 2" from the rounded nose edge. Fold on this line, right sides together. Slide the flat, open edge of the eye area into the fold. Stitch in place on the wrong side.

Step 8. Place two head pieces right sides together. Stitch around perimeter, leaving flat end open. Turn right side out. Position remaining U-shaped wire inside head/neck. Stuff head and very small portion of neck with polyester fiberfill. With 6-strand embroidery floss, embroider a mouth as shown on pattern.

Step 9. Place body on work surface, glue side up. Arrange four legs and head/neck as shown in Fig. 2. Glue in place and allow to

Fig. 2
Place legs and head/neck as shown.

dry thoroughly. Glue 4" medium green backing circle over joined areas. Allow to dry.

Step 10. Turn frog over and bend head up toward body. Glue in place.

Step 11. Tie a bow around neck with 1½"-wide soft green ribbon. Referring to photo, position two legs behind head and glue in place.

Step. 12. Referring to photo, position and glue medium-green beads on nose and legs. Glue craft eyes in place.

Step 13. Use cotton swab to apply cosmetic blush to cheeks. ✁

**"I'm So Cool" Frog Pincushion
Eye Area**
Cut 2 medium green

**"I'm So Cool" Frog Pincushion
Leg**
Cut 4 medium green
Cut 4 dark green
Enlarge pattern 125%

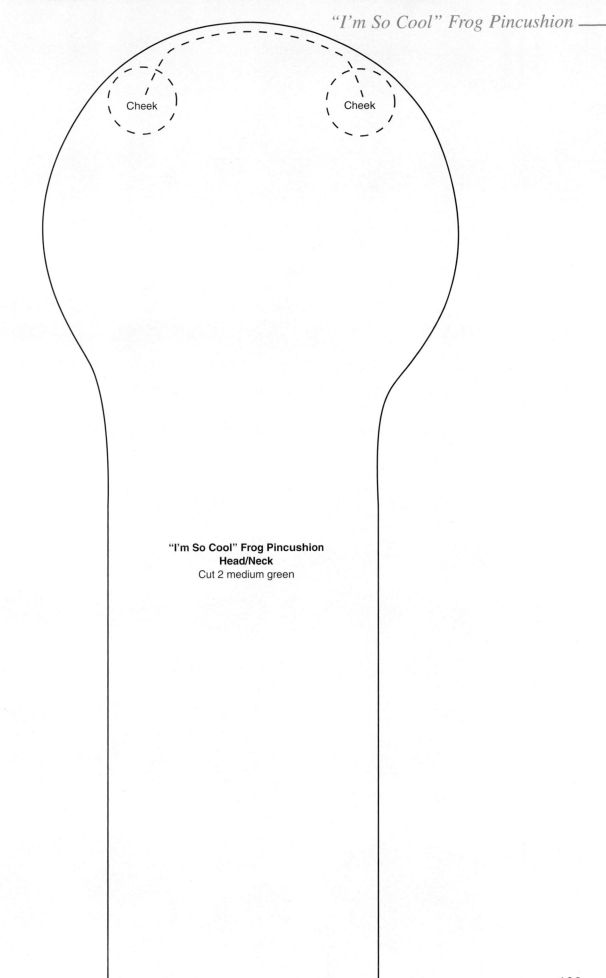

Cheek

Cheek

"I'm So Cool" Frog Pincushion
Head/Neck
Cut 2 medium green

The Backyard

Special times are often shared right in your own backyard while having a friendly chat with your neighbors or having family and friends over for an old-fashioned barbecue.

The projects in this chapter are perfect for decorating your patio, deck and backyard!

The best part of these projects? They're all made with scraps from your collection!

Sunflower Bucket

By Pearl Louise Krush

Create these colorful sunflowers and arrange them in a denim-covered bucket to add a touch of sunshine to your life—indoors or out!

Project Specifications

Skill Level: Beginner

Container Size: Approximately 5" x 12"

Sunflower Stems: 11" x 33"

Materials

- Yellow print scraps totaling ¼ yard for sunflower petals
- Burgundy print scraps totaling ¼ yard for sunflower centers
- Green print scraps totaling ¼ yard for sunflower leaves
- ⅝ yard denim for bucket cover
- 3 coordinating fabric strips 2½" x 42" for bucket trim
- Tin flower bucket approximately 5" x 12"
- Craft needle or safety pin
- 1 yard fusible transfer web
- 1 yard ⅛"-wide ribbon, any color
- 3 wooden dowel rods ¼" x 36"
- Dark green craft paint and paintbrush
- 2 (4") plastic foam balls
- Poster board or plastic scrap 4" x 4"
- 2 cups of weight product
- Piece of plastic foam for flower arranging to fit in lower portion of bucket
- Large handful of Spanish moss
- Low-temperature glue gun and glue
- All-purpose threads to match fabrics
- Basic sewing supplies and tools

Instructions

Step 1. Paint three wooden dowel sticks with dark green craft paint. Allow to dry thoroughly.

Step 2. From denim fabric cut one piece 8" taller than tin bucket and 1½ times the circumference. Bring long sides together, right sides facing, and sew seam. Fold one raw edge under 1" to form casing and sew around, leaving 1" opening at seam area.

Step 3. Thread craft needle with or insert safety pin in

⅛"-wide ribbon. Thread through 1" casing. Pull ribbon tightly until casing fits the bottom of the tin bucket. Knot ribbon and trim ends short. Turn right side out.

Step 4. Fold top raw edge of denim under to create a cuff at the top of the bucket. Fabric fold should extend approximately 1¼" above top rim of bucket.

Step 5. Fold one 2½" x 42" coordinating fabric strip lengthwise, bringing both raw edges to center, wrong sides facing; press. Bring two folded edges together so no raw edges are exposed; press. Repeat with remaining two strips. Pin three short ends of strips together and braid. Use low-temperature glue to secure strips at each end.

Step 6. Insert bucket in denim cover and tie braided strips around top of bucket, referring to photo for placement. Tuck the folded denim cuff to the inside. Glue cover to bucket at top and bottom to secure.

Step 7. Place weight product of choice in bottom of bucket. Insert plastic foam for flower arranging on top of weight material. Arrange Spanish moss on top.

Step 8. Trace flower petals and leaves on paper side of fusible transfer web as instructed on patterns. Cut out leaving roughly ¼" margin around traced lines. Fuse petals to wrong side of yellow print and leaves to wrong side of green print according to manufacturer's instructions. Cut out on traced lines.

Step 9. With matching thread, zigzag around outer edges of petals and leaves. Fold and glue a ½" pleat at the base of each petal.

Step 10. Cut the 4" plastic foam balls in half. (Discard one half.) Cut sunflower centers as directed on pattern. Place half-ball, round side down, in center of wrong side of fabric and pull fabric edges to flat side of ball. Push pins into fabric to secure.

Step 11. Arrange five petals around flat side of each ball, referring to photo for placement. Glue in place.

Step 12. Cut flower back and fabric cover as directed on pattern cover. Place flower back in center of wrong side of fabric cover. Pull fabric edges to reverse side of flower back and glue in place. Glue covered back circle to backside of each sunflower.

Step 13. Poke a hole through fabric and into plastic foam balls for dowel rods. Insert dowel rods and glue for stems.

Step 14. Fold base of each leaf around stem and glue as shown in Fig. 1. Glue three leaves to each stem.

Step 15. Insert three stems into plastic foam in bucket to finish. ✄

Fig. 1
Fold base of leaf to stick
and glue as shown.

**Sunflower Bucket
Sunflower Leaf**
Cut 9 green

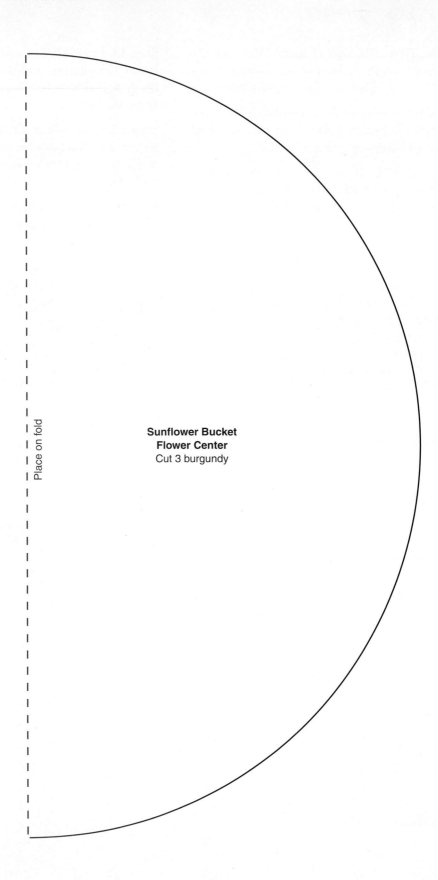

Place on fold

Sunflower Bucket
Flower Center
Cut 3 burgundy

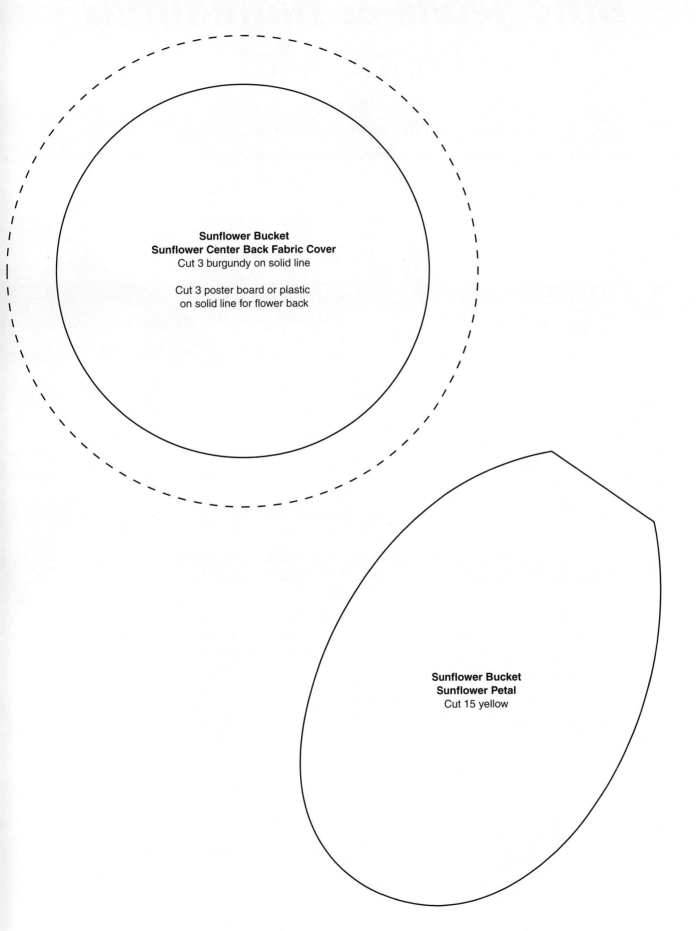

Sunflower Bucket
Sunflower Center Back Fabric Cover
Cut 3 burgundy on solid line

Cut 3 poster board or plastic
on solid line for flower back

Sunflower Bucket
Sunflower Petal
Cut 15 yellow

Blue Jeans & Bandannas Picnic Mat

By Kathy Brown

This is a great picnic accessory, and you can make it quickly and inexpensively with recycled items.

Project Specifications

Skill Level: Beginner

Picnic Mat Size: 36" x 36"

Napkin Size: 13" x 13"

Materials

- 4 squares 18½" x 18½" cut from recycled denim garments
- 4 pockets and 4 belt loops cut from recycled denim blue jeans
- 1 yard red bandanna fabric (or enough recycled bandanas to equal)
- Backing 38" x 38"
- Thin batting 38" x 38"
- All-purpose threads to match fabrics
- Basic sewing supplies and tools

Instructions

Step 1. Sew two 18½" denim squares together. Repeat with other two squares. Sew first pair to second pair to make a square 36½" x 36½".

Step 2. Referring to photo for placement, position each of the recycled denim pockets on each corner of denim square. Sew to the square following stitch lines on pocket. Leave open at top.

Step 3. Referring to photo for placement, position a belt loop to the left of each pocket. Sew to denim square at each end of each belt loop.

Step 4. Place backing face down on work surface and batting on top of it. Place denim square right side up on top. Pin-baste layers together. Stitch ¼" each side of center-cross seam lines to hold layers together. Trim all sides even with denim top.

Step 5. Cut and piece red bandanna fabric to make four binding strips 2" x 38". Cut four napkin squares 14" x 14".

Step 6. Right sides together, sew one binding strip to each side of denim square. Bring raw edges to back of denim square, fold edges under and hand-sew to finish sides and each end.

Step 7. Hem 14" x 14" bandanna squares and stuff into each pocket. Place picnic forks, knives and spoons in each of the belt loops. ✄

Woven Stripes Rug

By Pearl Louise Krush

Decorate outdoor woven rugs in any variety of colors and patterns to match seasonal themes. Your imagination is the limit!

Project Specifications

Skill Level: Beginner

Rug Size: Any size

Materials

- Woven sisal rug
- Scraps of each fabric color desired
- Large craft needle or safety pin
- Low-temperature glue gun and glue

Instructions

Step 1. Plan design and select fabric colors. See photo for one simple idea.

Step 2. Cut fabric scraps into 2½" strips. Fold long edges to center, wrong sides facing; press. Bring folded edges together again so no raw edges are exposed.

Step 3. Thread the end of first strip through the eye of the large craft needle or pin a safety pin to the end of a fabric strip. Weave the design of your choice through the weave of the mat. Leave fabric ends long enough to tie on the back of the rug.

Step 4. When weaving is complete, turn rug over and tie fabric ends together in knots. Cut ends short and glue to rug with low-temperature glue gun. ✄

Cowgirl Clothespin Corral

By Marian Shenk

Round up all those vagabond clothespins and keep
them under cover in this clever laundry room accessory.

Project Specifications

Skill Level: Beginner

Clothespin Corral Size: Approximately 17½" x 17½"

Materials

- ⅝ yard blue denim
- 2 red bandannas
- All-purpose thread to match fabrics
- 1 plastic clothes hanger
- Basic sewing supplies and tools

Instructions

Step 1. Cut denim as instructed on pattern. Place back and front pieces together, right sides facing, and sew shoulder seams with ¼" seam allowance.

Step 2. Cut arm trim as instructed on pattern. Place arm trim on right side of sleeve, wrong side of trim facing right side of bag, aligning outer raw edges. Press inner raw edges of trim under ¼" and topstitch in place.

Step 3. Cut front and back neck facings as instructed on patterns. Right sides facing and matching notches at the shoulders, sew back facing to front facings. Narrowly hem outer raw edge; press.

Step 4. Right sides together, pin facings to denim neck line and sew

with ¼" seam. Clip curved seam and press to wrong side. Sew bag center seam 6½" from top neckline opening to bag bottom.

Step 5. Cut an 8½" strip across the width of one bandanna. Run a gathering stitch along cut edge and pull up to fit across width of bag. Align bottom edge with bottom of bag. Sew to bag along gathering stitch.

Step 6. From solid red border of bandanna, cut a strip 1½" x 16". Right sides facing, align strip with upper edge of gathered bandanna. Sew across with ¼" seam. Fold strip up, fold raw edge under ¼" and topstitch to bag. Trim excess length even with sides of bag.

Step 7. Right sides facing and starting at facing edge of left shoulder, stitch all around perimeter of bag, returning to right shoulder facing.

Step 8. Turn bag right side out and insert plastic hanger through neck opening.

Step 9. From solid red border of bandanna cut a strip 2" x 10". Turn under ⅛" twice on each long edge of strip and topstitch to hem. Right sides facing, bring

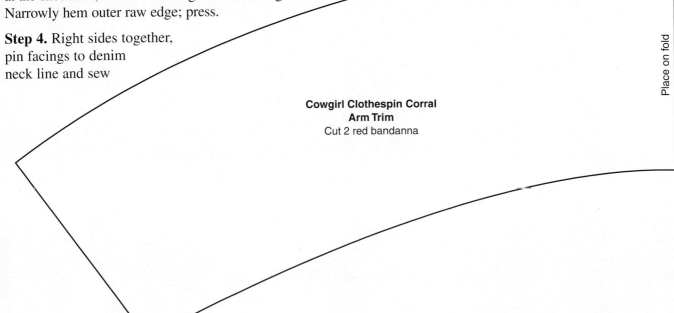

Cowgirl Clothespin Corral
Arm Trim
Cut 2 red bandanna

Place on fold

short raw ends together and stitch. Press ring flat with seam at center back.

Step 10. Cut 2" x 2½" strip from print portion of bandanna. Fold lengthwise, right sides together, and stitch. Turn right side out. Wrap around center of red ring to form a bow. Stitch ends together by hand and hand-tack to center front as shown in photo.

Step 11. Press facings back at center front to form lapels. ✂

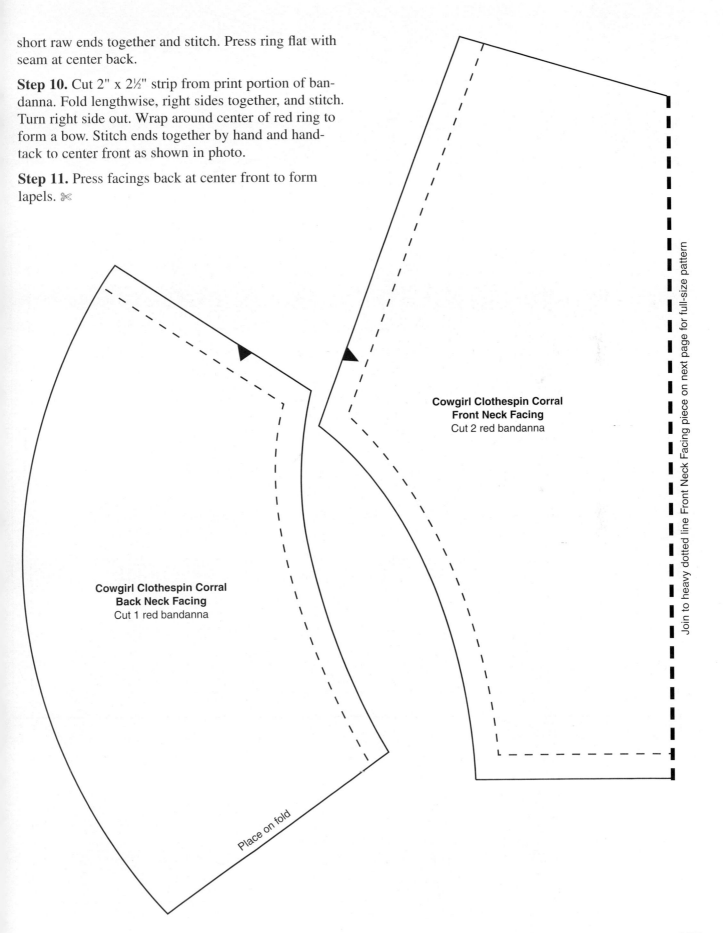

**Cowgirl Clothespin Corral
Front Neck Facing**
Cut 2 red bandanna

**Cowgirl Clothespin Corral
Back Neck Facing**
Cut 1 red bandanna

Place on fold

Join to heavy dotted line Front Neck Facing piece on next page for full-size pattern

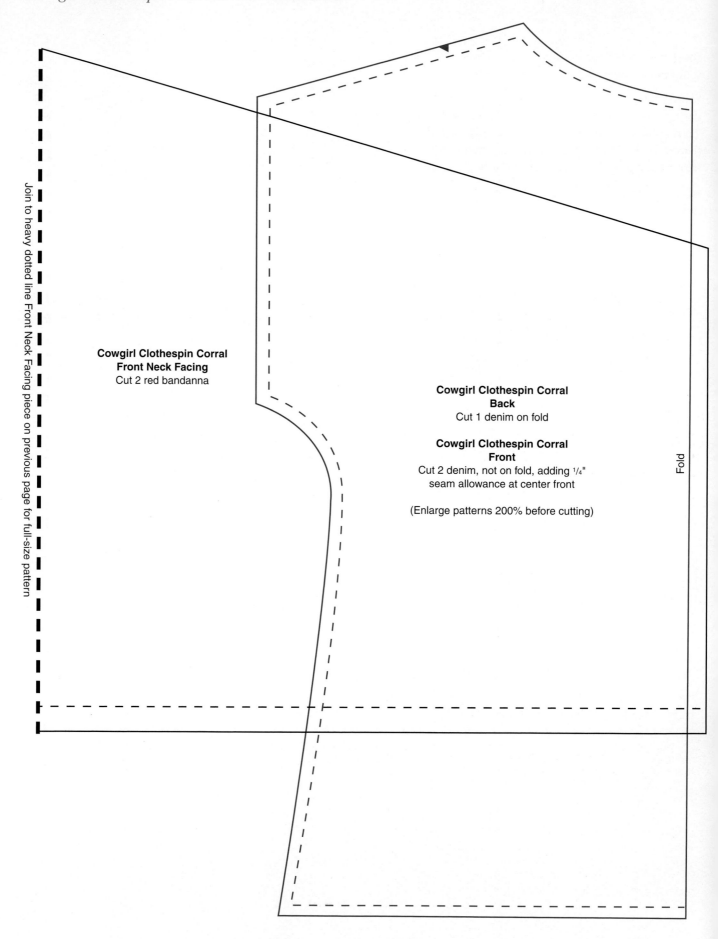

Join to heavy dotted line Front Neck Facing piece on previous page for full-size pattern

**Cowgirl Clothespin Corral
Front Neck Facing**
Cut 2 red bandanna

**Cowgirl Clothespin Corral
Back**
Cut 1 denim on fold

**Cowgirl Clothespin Corral
Front**
Cut 2 denim, not on fold, adding ¼"
seam allowance at center front

(Enlarge patterns 200% before cutting)

Fold

Cool Citrus Table Set

By Nancy Billetdeaux

What could be more delightfully crisp, cool and refreshing than citrus? Perfect for a summer table!

Project Specifications

Skill Level: Beginner

Place Mat Size: Approximately 19½" x 13½"

Napkin Size: 17" x 17"

Note: Materials and instructions are for two place mats and two napkins.

Materials

- ¾ yard prequilted white fabric
- ½ yard citrus green print fabric
- ½ yard citrus yellow print fabric
- 2 sheets 9" x 12" citrus green felt
- 2 sheets 9" x 12" citrus yellow felt
- ¼ yard fusible transfer web
- 10" piece (¾"-wide) elastic
- 2 (⅜") white buttons
- Pinking shears
- All-purpose threads to match fabrics
- Safety pins
- Pattern paper
- Basic sewing supplies and tools

Instructions

Step 1. Trace place mat on paper as instructed on pattern. Trace and cut fabric as directed.

Step 2. Place two place mat pieces right sides together and stitch around perimeter, leaving 6" opening. Turn right side out and close opening with hand stitches. Repeat for second place mat.

Step 3. Find centers of each place mat by folding in half. Mark with pin at top and bottom center. Fold the other direction and mark centers of sides.

Step 4. From prequilted white fabric cut circles as directed on pattern. From citrus green and citrus yellow felt cut circles as directed on pattern.

Step 5. Pin each white circle to one felt circle. Pin one green circle at each center mark of one place mat. Space and pin four green circles between each center circle. The circles should extend beyond the white place mat by about one-half the diameter of the circle. There will be one leftover circle. Reserve for the napkin ring. Repeat with yellow circles on second place mat.

Step 6. With white thread and large zigzag stitch, sew around each white circle. This will attach each white circle to the felt and the place mat.

Step 7. From citrus green and citrus yellow print fabrics cut one square each 18" x 18" and reserve for napkin. Cut one strip from each 3" x 15" and reserve for napkin ring.

Step 8. Following manufacturer's directions, fuse transfer web to back of each remaining piece of fabric. Trace 147 teardrop shapes each on paper backing of citrus green and yellow fabrics. Cut out on traced lines.

Step 9. Remove backing paper and arrange seven green teardrop shapes on each green felt-backed circle, referring to photo for placement; fuse. Repeat with yellow teardrop shapes on each yellow felt-backed circle; fuse. (Include circles reserved for napkin rings.)

Step 10. Fold the yellow 3" x 15" strip cut in Step 7 in half lengthwise, right sides together. Stitch long sides with ⅝" seam. Trim seam allowances and turn right side out with seam down center of backside; press.

Step 11. Cut ¾"-wide elastic in half and pin the safety pin in the end of one 5" elastic piece. Thread through yellow tube and pin to other end of tube with safety pin. Remove pins and stitch ends of elastic together.

Step 12. Fold elastic-covered tube in half with center seam up. Stitch through all thicknesses close to edge. Turn tube so center seam is inside. Stitch remaining citrus yellow circle to center of elastic-covered tube. Sew one white button to center of lemon slice.

Step 13. Repeat Steps 10–12 with green 3" x 15" strip cut in Step 7.

Step 14. Turn under ¼" on each side of yellow and green squares cut in Step 7; press. Turn under ¼" again and stitch to hem napkins.

Step 15. Fold and fan napkins and place each within matching napkin ring. ✄

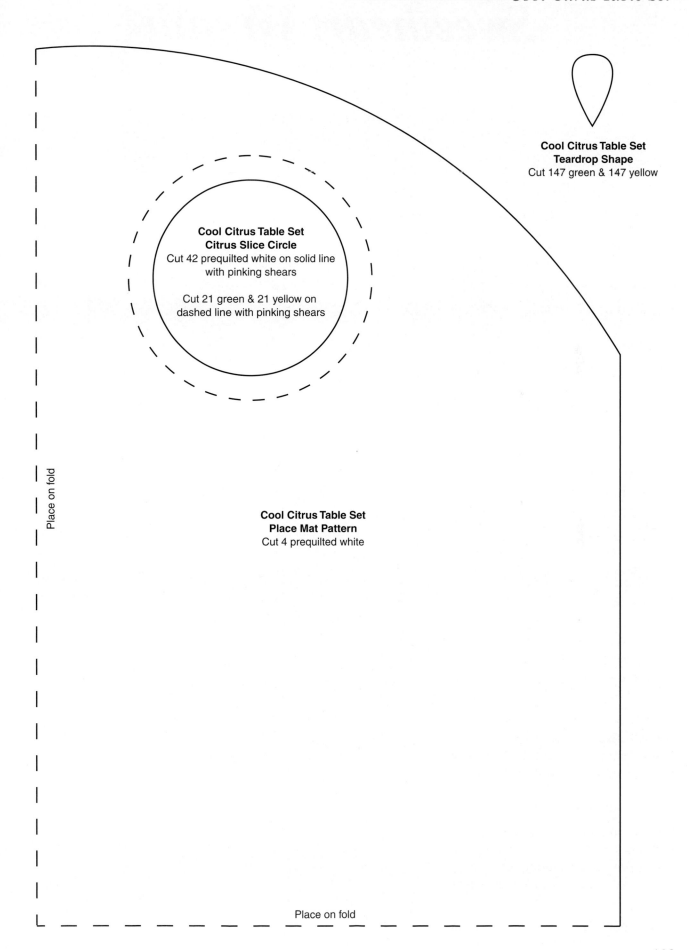

Cool Citrus Table Set
Teardrop Shape
Cut 147 green & 147 yellow

Cool Citrus Table Set
Citrus Slice Circle
Cut 42 prequilted white on solid line
with pinking shears

Cut 21 green & 21 yellow on
dashed line with pinking shears

Place on fold

Cool Citrus Table Set
Place Mat Pattern
Cut 4 prequilted white

Place on fold

Sweetheart Wreath

By June Fiechter

Designed to dress up your door, but you can hang this heart nearly anywhere in your house for a sweet accent.

Project Specifications

Skill Level: Beginner

Heart Wreath Size: Approximately 17" x 17"

Materials

- 2 squares of Kunin Kreative Kanvas 17" x 17"
- Thin craft batting 17" x 17"
- 3 strips of red fabric 3" x 24"
- 2 strips of peach fabric 3" x 20"
- 18 (⅝") craft berries with stems
- 4 light green silk multi-leafed stems
- 4 dark green silk leaves
- Wisps of Spanish moss
- White machine-quilting thread
- Fabric glue
- 4–6 small binder clips
- Dark rose craft spray paint
- Transparent tape
- 38" piece of ⅝"-wide coordinating plaid ribbon
- Basic sewing supplies and tools

Instructions

Step 1. Enlarge and trace heart pattern on each square of Kreative Kanvas. Cut out on traced lines. Use one heart to trace and cut heart from thin craft batting.

Step 2. Sandwich batting heart between two Kreative Kanvas hearts. Use binder clips to hold layers together. With white machine-quilting thread, sew double seams around inner and outer edges of heart ⅛" and ¼" from edges.

Step 3. On protected surface, spray both sides of heart with dark rose craft spray paint, concentrating on outer edges so that center of heart appears to be highlighted.

Step 4. Fold one of the fabric strips in

Sweetheart Wreath
Enlarge 200%

Place on fold

half lengthwise, wrong sides together. Sew raw edges together with a gathering stitch. Pull gathering thread as tightly as possible. Starting at one short end, roll the gathered fabric into a cylinder shape, keeping the gathered edges aligned. Wrap the gathered cylinder with transparent tape to hold shape. Place on work surface, gathered edges up. Apply fabric glue to all the raw edges and allow to dry. Repeat with all fabric strips.

Step 5. Reserve one dark green silk leaf and four

berries. Arrange and use fabric glue to attach the rest of the leaves and berries to center top of wreath. Incorporate fabric flowers in arrangement. Add wisps of Spanish moss. Nestle reserved berries and dark green leaf between flowers; glue.

Step 6. Cut ribbon into four 6" pieces and two 7" pieces. Make 6" pieces into loops and tuck randomly into arrangement; glue. Angle-cut ends of 7" ribbon pieces and tuck into arrangement. ✂

Folk Art Flag

By Willow Ann Sirch

Mix subtle plaids, checks and prints to achieve real folk art appeal for this banner. Let the stars dance on their field of blue for a little whimsy.

Project Specifications

Skill Level: Beginner

Flag Size: 21½" x 16½"

Materials

- 9 different blue checks and prints 3½" x 3½" for star backgrounds
- 3 different red strips 2" x 13"
- 3 different red strips 2" x 22"
- 3 different off-white shirting-type fabric strips 2" x 13"
- 2 different off-white shirting-type fabric strips 2" x 22"
- Variety of light scraps for stars
- ⅛ yard black-and-tan checked fabric for binding
- Backing 26" x 20"
- Thin batting 26" x 20"
- All-purpose threads to match fabrics
- 1 spool red hand-quilting thread
- Basic sewing supplies and tools

Instructions

Step 1. Trace and cut stars as directed on pattern. Clip inner angles and trim points for easier appliqué. Hand-appliqué one star to each 3½" blue background square. Angle each star slightly rather than lining up perfectly on square.

Step 2. Referring to photo for placement, alternate red and off-white 2" x 13" strips. Stitch together on long edges. Press seam allowances toward red strips. Repeat with 2" x 22" strips.

Step 3. Join three star squares in a row. Make three rows and join rows. Right sides together, sew star blocks to 13" joined red and off-white strips. Add joined 22" strips to lower edge of star/strip rectangle.

Step 4. Place backing fabric right side down on work surface. Place batting on backing. Center pieced flag on top. Pin or baste to secure layers for quilting.

Step 5. With red quilting thread, hand-quilt ¼" around each star and along one side of each stripe.

Trim batting and backing even with flag top.

Step 6. From black-and-tan checked fabric, cut two strips each 1¼" x 20" and 1¼" x 26" for binding.

Step 7. Place one long binding strip along lower edge of flag, one raw edge of binding aligned with raw edge of flag. Binding strip will extend about 2" at each end of flag. Sew to flag. Repeat for each side of flag.

Step 8. Miter corners by placing two loose binding ends of one corner right sides together. Mark and machine-sew with an X as shown in Fig. 1. Repeat at each corner. Trim excess fabric and flip binding around to back of flag. Fold raw edge under and hand-stitch in place with matching thread. ✂

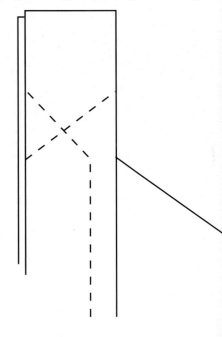

Fig. 1
Mark and machine-sew an X to miter each corner

Folk Art Flag Star
Cut 9 light

Autumn Leaves

By Mary Ayres

Bring those warm, paintbrush autumn colors right into your home with a variety of fabric scraps!

Project Specifications

Skill Level: Beginner

Pillow Size: 14" x 14"

Materials

- 4 different homespun squares 6½" x 6½" for backgrounds
- 14½" x 14½" pillow backing
- Gold, orange and green homespun scraps for leaves
- ⅛ yard tan checked fabric for borders
- 14" pillow form
- Black 6-strand embroidery floss and colors to match leaves
- Embroidery needle
- Water-soluble marker
- 1¾ yards jumbo black rickrack
- Scraps of fusible transfer web
- 9 (½") off-white recycled buttons
- Basic sewing supplies and tools

Instructions

Step 1. Sew 6½" homespun squares together in pairs and then join pairs as shown in Fig. 1.

Step 2. From tan checked fabric cut two strips each 1½" x 12½" and 1½" x 14½". Sew the shorter strips to two opposite sides of the assembled homespun squares. Sew longer strips to top and bottom.

Step 3. Trace leaf appliqués on paper side of fusible transfer web as directed on patterns. Cut out leaving roughly ¼" margin around traced lines. Following manufacturer's instructions, fuse shapes to selected fabrics; fuse. Cut out on traced lines.

Step 4. Referring to photo for placement, fuse each leaf to one homespun background square.

Step 5. With 3 strands of matching embroidery floss, work buttonhole stitch around each leaf. Transfer stems and veins to leaves. Embroider stems and veins with 3 strands of black embroidery floss, using stem stitch.

Step 6. Sew one off-white button to each corner of each homespun background square with black embroidery floss. Stitch with parallel stitches rather than X's, and make stitches of all buttons run the same direction.

Step 7. Sew jumbo black rickrack around perimeter of pillow on the right side ¼" from edge. Start and finish at one corner. Sew through center of rickrack.

Step 8. Right sides together, sew pillow top to pillow backing along previous rickrack stitches. Leave an 11" opening at bottom. Turn right side out. Insert pillow form and close opening with hand stitches. ✂

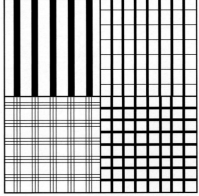

Fig. 1
Join homespun squares as shown

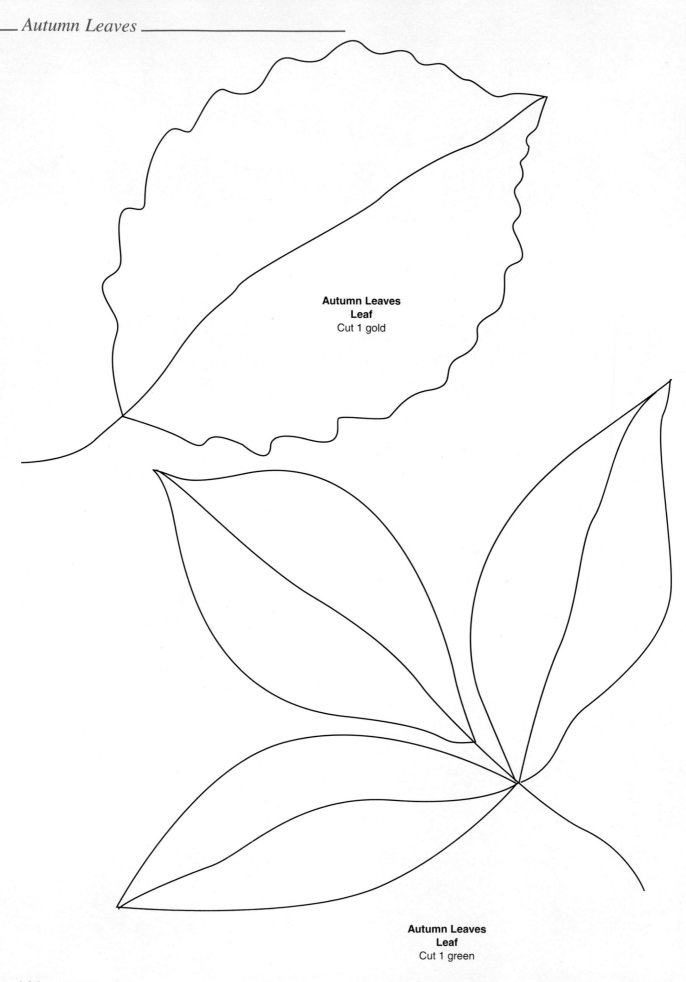

**Autumn Leaves
Leaf**
Cut 1 gold

**Autumn Leaves
Leaf**
Cut 1 green

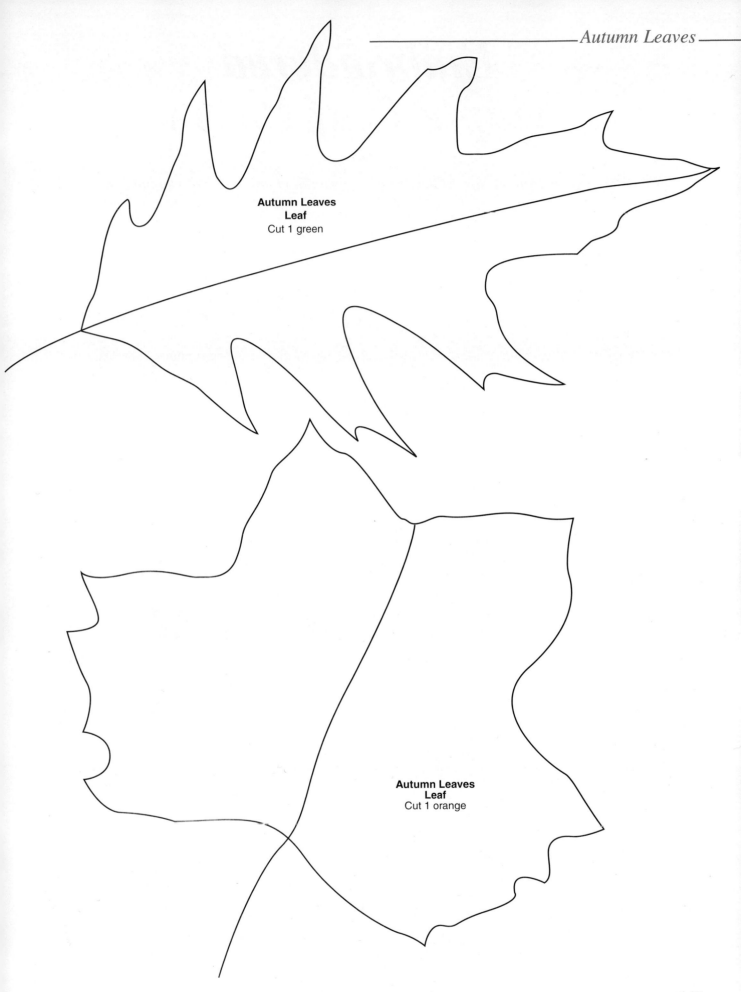

**Autumn Leaves
Leaf**
Cut 1 green

**Autumn Leaves
Leaf**
Cut 1 orange

Embroidered Maple Leaf Pillow

By Mary Ayres

Use themes from nature to inspire rich seasonal changes in your home decor.

Project Specifications

Skill Level: Beginner

Pillow Size: 14" x 14"

Materials

- 10½" x 10½" square light green mottled or solid fabric for design background
- ½ yard dark green check for borders and backing
- 1¾ yards light green cord piping
- Dark green 6-strand embroidery floss
- Embroidery needle
- Water-soluble marker
- 14" pillow form
- Basic sewing supplies and tools

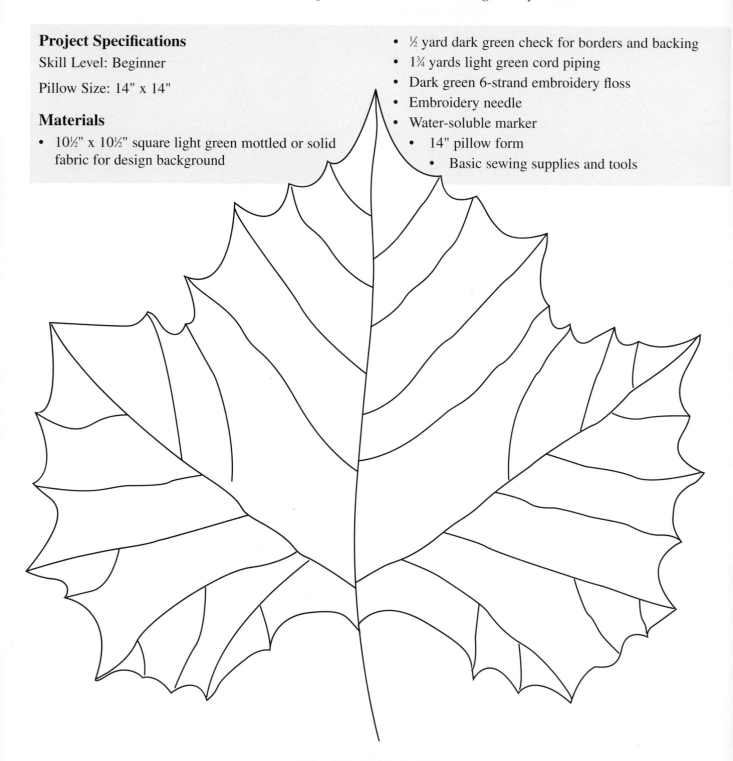

Embroidered Maple Leaf Pillow
Maple Leaf Pattern
Enlarge 125%

Instructions

Step 1. From dark green check cut two strips each 2½" x 10½" and 2½" x 14½". Sew the shorter strips to two opposite sides of the 10½" x 10½" light green mottled or solid fabric square. Sew the longer strips to the top and bottom. Press seam allowances toward borders.

Step 2. Trace maple leaf pattern on light green center square. With 2 strands of dark green embroidery floss, embroider outline and all details with stem stitch.

Step 3. Sew light green cord piping around perimeter of pillow on front side ¼" from edge, beginning and ending in a bottom corner. Clip piping at corners as you sew.

Step 4. From dark green check cut one square 14½" x 14½" for backing. Right sides together, sew to pillow top along previous cording stitches. Leave an 11" opening at bottom. Turn right side out. Insert pillow form and close opening with hand stitches. ✂

The Christmas Home

The excitement of Christmas comes every year, and with this excitement comes decorating your home to make it warm and welcoming for friends and loved ones. You've been waiting for just the right design to use up some Christmas fabric scraps, and we have just the right one in this chapter!

While getting ready to sew your next scrap project, take a few moments to just sit back and sip a cup of hot chocolate! Ahhh, how good it feels to relax. Happy Holidays!

Jolly St. Nick Stocking

By Kathleen Hurley

This small stocking goes together quickly with very few materials,
and it's just the right size to hold special little gifts

Project Specifications

Skill Level: Beginner

Stocking Size: Approximately 8" x 11½"

Materials

- 1 felt square each dark green and white
- Scraps of medium green, red, cream and rose
- 6-strand embroidery floss in burgundy, medium blue, white, black, medium green and cream
- 2 yards ¼"-wide metallic gold cord
- Water-soluble marker
- Paper punch (optional to cut holly berries)
- Fabric glue (optional)
- Basic sewing supplies and tools

Instructions

Step 1. Trace pattern and cut stocking front as directed. From white felt cut stocking cuff 2" x 5⅜". Place cuff overlapping stocking front ¼" and stitch in place.

Step 2. Place stocking top on white felt and trace around shape. Cut out on traced line for stocking back.

Step 3. Trace all appliqué pieces on felt with water-soluble marker. Cut out pieces, immerse in cool water to remove marker and allow to dry thoroughly. Press with cool iron.

Step 4. Referring to assembly diagram and photo, place appliqué pieces in their numbered order, securing each in place with pins, fabric glue or basting.

Step 5. Hand-appliqué each piece (except holly leaves and holly berries) in place with 1 strand of matching embroidery floss.

Step 6. With 2 strands of burgundy embroidery floss embroider inner mouth with satin stitch. Embroider eyes with satin stitch and 2 strands of medium blue embroidery floss, then 2 strands of black embroidery floss. Highlight each eye with a single French knot worked with 2 strands of white embroidery floss.

Step 7. Attach each holly leaf to stocking with a vein line of outline stitch worked through all layers. Edges of leaves are loose. Attach each holly berry to stocking with a single French knot, using 2 strands of red embroidery floss. Edges are loose.

Step 8. Sew metallic gold cord to stocking front along bottom of cuff. Tack ends of braid behind stocking front.

Step 9. Place assembled stocking front on stocking back, aligning all edges. Leaving top open, stitch layers together with 1 strand of white embroidery floss. Place metallic gold cord along all outside edges of stocking and secure with a single strand of white embroidery floss.

Step 10. Cut an 8" piece of metallic gold cord. Bring short ends together to make a hanging loop. Attach ends to stocking inside cuff.

Project Note: If you would like to personalize stocking, draw outline of cuff on tracing paper and cut out. Write name on pattern. Place pattern on cuff and secure with basting stitches. Working through paper, stitch name with outline stitch and 2 strands of embroidery floss in color of your choice. ✄

Continued on page 172

Christmas Cardinals

By Diana Stunell-Dunsmore

Whether made au naturel or dressed in tiny outfits, this flock of cardinals will make a bright addition to the Christmas scene.

Project Specifications

Skill Level: Beginner

Cardinal Size: Each approximately 4" in height or length

Note: All cardinals are sewn by hand. There is some machine-sewing on cardinal clothing. Materials are for entire set of five designs.

Materials

- 2 squares red felt
- Scraps of black and yellow felt
- White and sturdy denim-type green fabric scraps
- 7" scrap of narrow red rickrack
- 4" piece of ⅛"-wide red satin ribbon
- 8" piece of ⅛"-wide white satin ribbon
- 2" piece of ¼"-wide white satin ribbon
- 16" piece of ¹⁄₁₆"-wide green satin ribbon
- 16" piece of clear fishing line or nylon monofilament
- 2 white seed beads
- 9 black seed beads
- Black 6-strand embroidery floss
- Long embroidery needle
- Red, black, yellow, white and green all-purpose thread
- Hot-glue gun and glue
- Fabric glue
- Polyester fiberfill
- 2 pieces off-white card stock 2" x 3"
- Black, brown and green fine-point permanent markers
- Basic sewing supplies and tools

Instructions

Boy Cardinal

Step 1. From red felt cut two Dressed Cardinal bodies, one Dressed Cardinal gusset, four Cardinal wings, two Dressed Cardinal tails and one base. From black felt cut one face patch. From yellow felt cut one each: upper beak, lower beak and center beak. From card stock cut 1 base.

Step 2. Glue card-stock base to red felt base. Set aside to dry.

Step 3. With matching thread whipstitch back seams of body pieces together. Whipstitch one side of gusset to one side of body front from base to top point of head. Continue to stitch gusset to other side of body from top of head down to base.

Step 4. Stuff body firmly with polyster fiberfill. Whipstitch glued base, felt side out, to bottom of body.

Step 5. Whipstitch two wings together, stuffing lightly as you go. Repeat for second wing. Do not embroider lines on wings.

Step 6. Place two tail pieces together. Embroider black line with 1 strand of black embroidery floss by using a running stitch through both layers. Reverse running stitch at end of line and fill between previous stitches (filled-in running stitch). Hide knots between layers.

Step 7. Whipstitch layers around long sides and wide end of tail. Gather short end as tightly as possible and knot. Set aside.

Step 8. Embroider lines on sides of head using same filled-in running stitch. Use long needle and enter and end through face, which will later be covered, to hide knots.

Step 9. Sew black seed beads in place for eyes, again hiding knots where beak will be.

Step 10. Referring to photo, whipstitch black face in place (wider part is lower half).

Step 11. With matching thread whipstitch upper beak to center beak along rounded edges, matching center dots. Whipstitch lower beak to straight edge on bottom of center beak. Stuff upper and lower beak as firmly as possible and pin in place over black face patch. Whipstitch beak in place.

Step 12. Whipstitch wings to body, straight edge forming top of wing.

Step 13. From sturdy denim-type green fabric cut one overall bib and one overall pants. Fold bib right sides together and stitch sides with ⅛" seam allowance. Turn right side out through bottom edge; press. Topstitch about ⅛" from three closed edges. Sew one white seed bead at two upper corners of topstitching.

Step 14. Topstitch pockets, zipper, center and side seams as marked on pattern, using a very close zigzag and matching thread. Press under ¼" on upper and lower edges. Topstitch through both thicknesses at lower edge to hem. Match right side of bib to wrong side of pants at upper edge and topstitch hem through all layers and attaching bib. Right sides together, sew back seam of pants. Finger-press seam allowance to one side.

Step 15. Place overalls on cardinal. Hot-glue bib to chest. Hand-stitch tail to back seam of overalls ¼" down from top.

Step 16. Make a small bow tie from ¼"-wide white ribbon, hiding raw edges. Wrap white thread around center to form tie shape. Sew or glue to cardinal above overall bib.

Girl Cardinal

Step 1. Repeat Boy Cardinal Steps 1–12 to make bird.

Step 2. From white scraps cut apron 6" x 1¾" and one apron bib. Fold bib right sides together and stitch sides

with narrow seam allowance. Turn right side out through bottom edge; press.

Step 3. Turn short ends of apron under ⅛" and topstitch. Press one long edge under ¼" twice and topstitch to hem; press. With red thread sew narrow rickrack over previous hem-stitching line. Fold ends of rickrack to backside.

Step 4. Press under ¼" on remaining raw edge of apron. Sew a gathering thread through both layers and pull up to fit around waist of bird, just under wings. Hot-glue bib to bird's chest. Hand-stitch or glue apron to bird, leaving a small opening at back for tail. Hand-stitch tail in place just below waist.

Step 5. With 4" lengths of red and white ⅛"-wide ribbon, tie two tiny white bows and one red. With fabric glue attach one white bow to side of head along seam, one white bow at apron closure just above tail and red bow to apron bib.

Fat Cardinal Ornament

Step 1. From red felt cut two Cardinal Ornament bodies, one Cardinal Ornament gusset, four Cardinal Ornament wings and two Cardinal Ornament tails. From black felt cut one face patch. From yellow felt cut one each: upper beak, lower beak and center beak and two feet.

Step 2. With matching thread whipstitch back seams of body pieces together. Whipstitch gusset to one side of cardinal from top of head, around bottom of body to tail. Repeat for other side, stuffing firmly with polyester fiberfill as you go.

Step 3. Embroider stitches on head as in Boy Cardinal, Step 8. Add eyes as in Step 9. Add black face patch as in Step 10. Make and add beak as in Step 11. Make wings as in Step 5.

Step 4. With 1 strand of black embroidery floss, embroider lines on one wing as in Step 6, Boy

Fig. 1
Reverse embroidery on wings as shown.

Cardinal. Reverse for second wing as shown in Fig. 1. Hand-stitch or glue wings to body, following placement lines on pattern.

Step 5. With black embroidery floss work same running stitch on each tail piece, hiding knots on back of each piece. Whipstitch two tail pieces together on two long sides and across wide end, stuffing lightly as you go. Fold short open end of tail in half, matching corners, and stitch to hold. Stitch fold securely to body.

Step 6. Glue feet to bottom of body.

Step 7. Tie 8" piece of ¹⁄₁₆"-wide green satin ribbon around cardinal's neck and form a bow.

Step 8. Thread 8" length of clear fishing line or nylon

monofilament through upper point of head. Tie to form hanging loop. Cardinal will hang straight and balanced.

Flat Cardinal Ornament

Step 1. From red felt cut two Cardinal Ornament bodies, two Cardinal Ornament wings and two Flat Cardinal Ornament tails. From black felt cut two Flat Cardinal Ornament face patches. From yellow felt cut two Flat Ornament Cardinal beaks.

Step 2. Lightly glue right side of one beak seam allowance to wrong side of corresponding cardinal face. Use only enough glue to hold in place until sewn. Repeat for other beak and cardinal piece. Be sure pieces will align perfectly when sewn together later.

Step 3. Make tail as in Step 6, Boy Cardinal, but sew layers together with simple running stitch.

Step 4. Embroider lines in each single-layer wing, reversing stitching direction as shown on Fig. 1.

Step 5. With black thread, backstitch face patches to corresponding cardinal pieces between face and beak. Embroider lines on beak and sides of head with 1 strand of black embroidery floss in a backstitch or filled-in running stitch. Sew two black seed beads on for eyes.

Step 6. Stitch two sides together starting at underside of beak using yellow thread and filled-in running stitch to stitch beaks together. With black thread take a couple of stitches through face patches. With red thread, starting above beak, sew with a simple running stitch all around cardinal, stuffing lightly as you go. Remember to insert tail at end of back and sew through all four layers.

Step 7. Glue wrong side of each wing to right sides of bird.

Step 8. Thread 8" length of clear fishing line or nylon monofilament through upper point of head. Tie to form hanging loop. Tie 8" piece of ¹⁄₁₆"-wide green satin ribbon around cardinal's neck and form a bow.

Fig. 2
Draw pine branch and needles
on card stock as shown.

Cardinal Gift Tag

Step 1. From red felt cut one Gift Tag cardinal and one Gift Tag wing. From yellow felt cut one Gift Tag beak.

Step 2. With black, brown and green fine-point permanent markers draw a small pine branch and needles on 2" x 3" card stock as shown in Fig. 2.

Step 3. With 1 strand of black embroidery floss straight-stitch lines on cardinal body, tail, beak and wing. Satin-stitch face patch. Sew on one black seed bead eye.

Step 4. Referring to photo for placement, glue cardinal body and beak to pine branch. Glue wing to cardinal. With 2 strands of green embroidery floss tie a tiny bow and glue to cardinal's throat. ✄

**Dressed Cardinal
Tail**

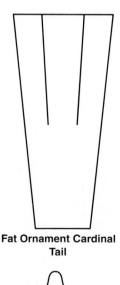

**Fat Ornament Cardinal
Tail**

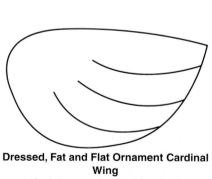

**Dressed, Fat and Flat Ornament Cardinal
Wing**
(Omit lines on Dressed Cardinal)

**Gift Tag Cardinal
Wing**

**Flat Ornament Cardinal
Face Patch**

**Flat Ornament Cardinal
Tail**

**Ornament Cardinal
Foot**

**Dressed & Ornament Cardinal
Center Beak**

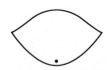

**Dressed & Ornament Cardinal
Upper Beak**

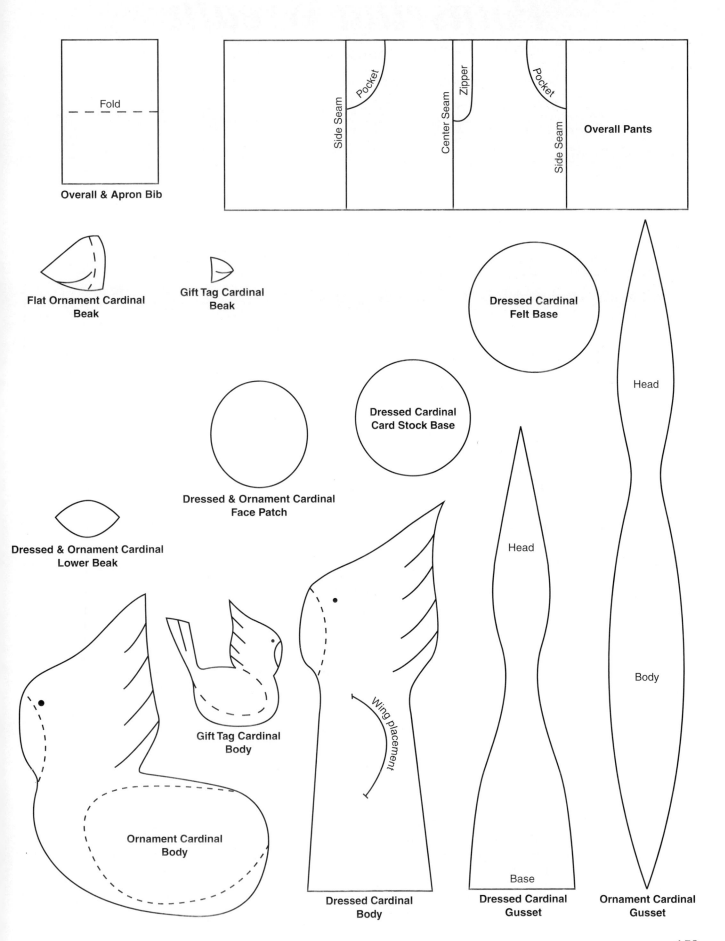

Fold

Overall & Apron Bib

Side Seam

Pocket

Center Seam

Zipper

Pocket

Side Seam

Overall Pants

Flat Ornament Cardinal Beak

Gift Tag Cardinal Beak

Dressed Cardinal Felt Base

Head

Dressed & Ornament Cardinal Lower Beak

Dressed & Ornament Cardinal Face Patch

Dressed Cardinal Card Stock Base

Head

Body

Gift Tag Cardinal Body

Wing placement

Ornament Cardinal Body

Body

Dressed Cardinal Body

Base

Dressed Cardinal Gusset

Ornament Cardinal Gusset

Poinsettia Wreath

By Charlyne Stewart

This sparkling fabric wreath will become part of your annual
Christmas collection to be used in your home year after year.

Project Specifications

Skill Level: Beginner

Wreath Size: Approximately 12" diameter

Materials

- 12" plastic foam full-round wreath form
- ⅔ yard green/gold metallic print
- ½ yard red/gold metallic print
- ½ yard dark green print
- ¾ yard thin batting
- Red, green and yellow all-purpose sewing thread
- 1 spool gold metallic thread
- 4" piece of green single-fold bias tape
- 1 package gold sequins
- 1 package gold seed beads
- Straight pins
- Fabric glue
- Sewing machine with walking foot
- Freezer paper
- Recycled manila folder
- Water-soluble marker
- Basic sewing supplies and tools

Instructions

Step 1. Trace petal and leaf patterns on paper side of freezer paper. Cut out leaving roughly ¼" around shapes. Iron shapes to recycled manila folder and cut out on traced lines for templates.

Step 2. Fold red/gold metallic print in half, right sides facing. Place on top of thin batting. Pin at frequent intervals. Trace 18 petals with template made in Step 1. Cut out each unit on traced lines.

Step 3. Repeat Step 2 with green/gold print metallic and trace 16 leaves. Cut out on traced lines.

Step 4. Stitch around each petal and leaf with matching threads and a ⅛" seam allowance. Leave open between dots for turning. Turn each right side out and close opening with hand stitches.

Step 5. With water-soluble marker trace vein lines on each petal and leaf. With walking foot and large stitch, quilt vein lines with gold metallic thread in needle and yellow thread in bobbin.

Step 6. From dark green print tear six 2½" strips across the width of the fabric. Wrap the plastic foam wreath with overlapping fabric strips, pinning edges with straight pins pressed directly into foam and gluing ends. Remove pins when glue is dry.

Step 7. Arrange quilted green leaves on front of

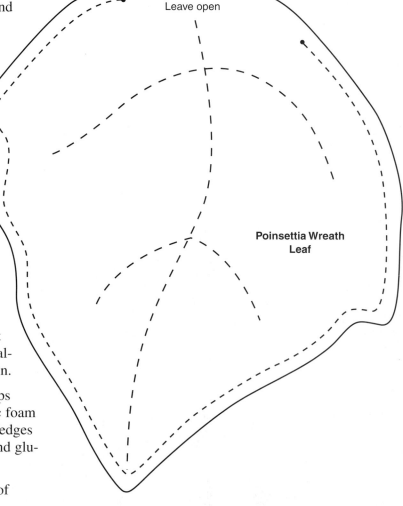

Leave open

Poinsettia Wreath
Leaf

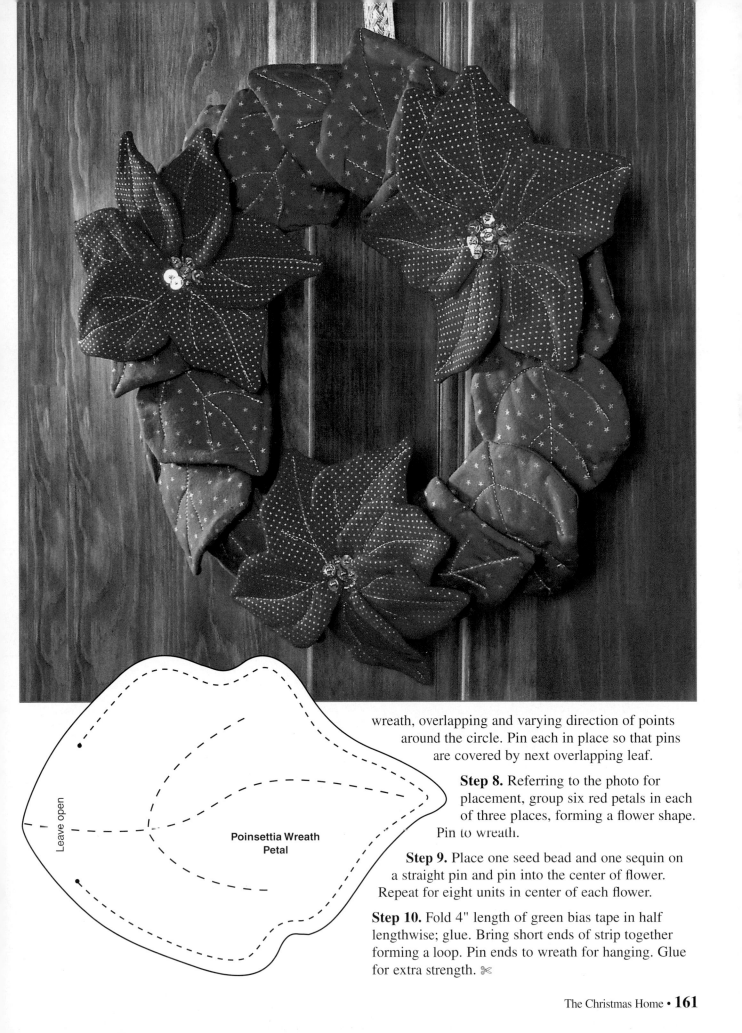

Leave open

Poinsettia Wreath Petal

wreath, overlapping and varying direction of points around the circle. Pin each in place so that pins are covered by next overlapping leaf.

Step 8. Referring to the photo for placement, group six red petals in each of three places, forming a flower shape. Pin to wreath.

Step 9. Place one seed bead and one sequin on a straight pin and pin into the center of flower. Repeat for eight units in center of each flower.

Step 10. Fold 4" length of green bias tape in half lengthwise; glue. Bring short ends of strip together forming a loop. Pin ends to wreath for hanging. Glue for extra strength. ✄

Christmas Tree Gift Bag

By Mary Ayres

Make the contents even more special by presenting your gift in a terrifically personalized bag.

Project Specifications

Skill Level: Beginner

Gift Bag Size: Approximately 4" x 16½" x 2"

Materials

- 2 rectangles blue glitter fabric 6½" x 18¼"
- Scraps of green, yellow and brown for appliqué
- Black 6-strand embroidery floss
- 1 (¾") red button
- 1 yard ¼"-wide red satin ribbon
- ¾ yard 2"-wide gold wire-edged ribbon
- Embroidery needle
- Safety pin
- Scraps of fusible transfer web
- Basic sewing supplies and tools

Instructions

Step 1. Trace a 1½" x 7¼" rectangle and tree and star shapes on paper side of fusible transfer web. Cut out leaving roughly ¼" margin around traced lines. Following manufacturer's instructions fuse rectangle to brown scrap for tree trunk, and tree and star to selected fabrics. Cut out on traced lines.

Step 2. Referring to photo for placement, center appliqué shapes on right side of one blue glitter rectangle; fuse.

Step 3. With 3 strands of black embroidery floss, work buttonhole stitch around appliqué shapes.

Step 4. Tie 2"-wide gold wire-edged ribbon into shapely bow and trim ends. Attach to tree trunk 1½" down from bottom of tree. Sew ¾" red button through all layers.

Step 5. Right sides facing, sew the two blue glitter rectangles together on both sides and bottom. Leave ½" opening ¾"

Christmas Tree Gift Bag
Christmas Tree
Cut 1 green

down from top of bag on one side to insert ribbon in casing.

Step 6. Align bottom and side seams and press bag flat. Stitch across bottom of bag 1" from each of the corners as shown in Fig. 1 to form box bottom of bag. Turn bag right side out.

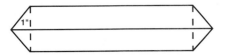

Fig. 1
Stitch across bottom of bag as shown.

Step 7. Press raw edges under ¾" at top of bag. Turn raw edge under ¼" and sew around top of bag close to turned raw edge to form casing.

Step 8. Insert safety pin in end of ¼"-wide red ribbon. Insert in opening of casing and work through casing back to opening. Insert gift in bag. Pull ribbons up evenly into a bow, gathering the top of the bag casing. ✀

Christmas Tree Gift Bag
Star
Cut 1 yellow

Bluework Snowman

By Mary Ayres

*Perfect for that little something that you'd like
to give a teacher, friend or special person in your life.*

Project Specifications

Skill Level: Beginner

Size: 9" x 11"

Materials

- White rectangle 5½" x 7½"
- 2 strips each blue print 2½" x 5½" and 2½" x 7½"
- 4 squares bright blue solid 2½" x 2½"
- Backing 10" x 12"
- Thin batting 10" x 12"
- 1¼ yards dark blue piping
- 1 skein bright blue 6-strand embroidery floss
- Embroidery needle
- Water-soluble marker
- All-purpose threads to match fabrics
- 4 (¾") white buttons
- Basic sewing supplies and tools

Instructions

Step 1. Sew 2½" x 7½" blue print strips to long sides of white rectangle. Sew 2½" x 2½" bright blue squares to each end of 2½" x 5½" blue print strips. Sew to top and bottom of center panel.

Step 2. Transfer snowman pattern to center of white center panel. Use stem stitch and 1 strand of bright blue embroidery floss to embroider snowman. Embroider French knots on eye and mouth, wrapping floss around needle three times.

Step 3. Trim batting and backing to same size as embroidered panel. Baste batting to back of panel. Sew dark blue piping around front side of panel, ¼" from edge, beginning and ending at a bottom corner. Clip piping seam at corners as you sew.

Step 4. Right sides facing, sew top panel to backing, stitching along previous piping stitches. Leave 4" opening at bottom for turning. Turn right side out and close opening with hand stitches.

Step 5. Sew one white button to center of each border corner square with bright blue embroidery floss. Stitch through all layers with an X through buttonholes. ✂

Bluework Snowman Pattern

String of Lights Candle Mat

By Holly Daniels

Quick and easy design for Christmas craft fair, gift-giving or decorating your own home. You'll want to make more than one!

Project Specifications

Skill Level: Beginner

Candle Mat Size: 18" diameter

Materials

- 19" x 19" square of green plaid
- 13" x 13" square of white-on-white
- Scraps of red, blue, green and yellow
- Backing 20" x 20"
- Thin batting 20" x 20"
- 1 package red jumbo rickrack
- ½ yard string
- 1¼ yards black soutache braid
- 1⅔ yards red purchased or self-made bias binding
- All-purpose threads to match fabrics
- Water-soluble marker
- Freezer paper
- Basic sewing supplies and tools

Instructions

Step 1. Fold 19" x 19" green plaid square twice. Press lightly. Using water-soluble marker, mark 9" points as shown in Fig. 1. Tie string to marker. Hold loose end of string at corner and place marker on one of the side marks. Using the marker like a compass, draw a quarter circle. Cut out on marked line.

Step 2. Fold, press and mark white 13" x 13" square as shown in Fig. 2. Mark and cut as in Step 1 for a 3"-wide ring.

Step 3. Center white ring on green plaid circle. Align the folds; pin. Sew around both edges of white ring; press. Working carefully from wrong side of circle, cut away green plaid from under white ring leaving narrow seam allowance.

Step 4. Trace light bulb on paper side of freezer paper 12 times. Cut out bulb shapes and place waxy side down on wrong side of red, green, blue and yellow scraps, leaving roughly ¼" around each shape. Press raw edges of each appliqué to paper side of bulb shape.

Step 5. Referring to photo for placement, pin each bulb in place on white ring. Hand-appliqué with matching thread. Leave one bulb partially unstitched at top. You may remove freezer paper when each bulb is nearly stitched, or it can be removed from the back of the white ring when all stitching is complete by cutting a small slit in the white fabric behind each bulb.

Step 6. Insert one end of black soutache braid into unstitched end of one bulb. Tack in place by hand. Referring to photo, wind braid around between bulbs, making an occasional curl and curve. Be sure braid lies flat. Pin as you go. When you reach the starting point, cut braid slightly longer than needed and insert back into the open end of the bulb. Tack in place. Sew braid to mat by hand or machine. Close open end of bulb with hand stitches.

Continued on page 171

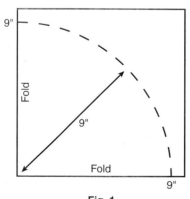

Fig. 1
Mark 9" points as shown.

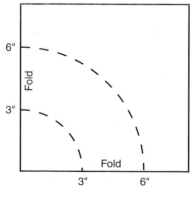

Fig. 2
Mark 3" and 6" points as shown.

Light Bulb
Cut 12 freezer paper

Kris Moose

By Chris Malone

Guaranteed to bring a twinkle to the eye and a giggle from the beholder.

Project Specifications

Skill Level: Beginner

Wall Quilt Size: 14½" x 16"

Materials

- 11" x 12½" piece of muslin or osnaburg
- Scraps of light and medium brown for appliqué
- ¼ yard green print for first border and tabs
- ⅛ yard red solid for second border
- ½ yard red-and-green Christmas print for outer border and backing
- Black 6-strand embroidery floss
- Embroidery needle and hoop
- Scraps of fusible transfer web
- Thin batting 16" x 18"
- Red, green and ecru quilting thread
- 2 (⅜") black buttons
- 1 (⅞") black button
- 2 (1¼") black buttons
- Water-soluble marker
- 1" x 18" wooden slat
- 2 (1½") wooden cutout craft trees
- 2 (¾") wooden cutout craft stars
- Dark green, medium green and gold acrylic paints
- Paintbrush
- Small sponge or stencil brush
- Wood glue
- Walnut stain and satin varnish
- Black fine-line permanent marker
- 2 small sawtooth hangers
- Basic sewing supplies and tools

Instructions

Step 1. With pencil mark a 9" x 10 ½" rectangle on muslin or osnaburg. Trace words from pattern onto fabric with water-soluble marker. Tape pattern to window or light table and center fabric over design.

Step 2. Place marked fabric in embroidery hoop. With 2 strands of black embroidery floss, backstitch letters and make French knots for dots.

Step 3. Trace antler, ear and face appliqué shapes on paper side of fusible transfer web. Cut out leaving roughly ¼" outside traced lines. Following manufacturer's instructions, fuse to selected fabrics. Refer to photo for colors. Cut out on traced lines.

Step 4. Referring to pattern and photo, arrange and fuse appliqué shapes to background. Using 2 strands of black embroidery floss, work buttonhole stitch around all raw edges. Backstitch mouth. Do not sew buttons on, but mark placement. Make two straight stitches above for eyebrows.

Step 5. Trim background piece to marked pencil lines.

Step 6. Cut 1½" strip across width of green print. Sew strip to top and bottom of background, trimming even with ends. Repeat with sides of piece, trimming even. Press seam allowances toward border.

Step 7. From red solid cut two ¾" strips across width of fabric. Sew to center unit as in Step 6.

Step 8. From red-and-green Christmas print cut two 2½" strips across width of fabric. Sew to center unit as in Steps 6 and 7.

Step 9. Place batting on flat surface and smooth out any wrinkles or bumps. Place red-and-green Christmas print right side up on top of batting. Place pieced center right side down on top of backing. Pin through all layers to secure. Cut batting and backing even with top.

Step 10. Sew around perimeter, leaving 5" opening at center bottom. Trim batting close to seam. Turn right side out and close opening with hand stitches.

Step 11. Pin or baste through centers of each border to secure for quilting. With matching thread colors, quilt in the ditch along each seam.

Step 12. From green print cut two pieces 4½" x 8½" for hanging loops. Fold each in half lengthwise, right sides together, and sew along raw edges of each, leaving 2" opening in one side. Clip corners, turn right side out; press.

Step 13. Fold one loop over top of quilt, 3" from corner and overlapping top edge 1½" front and back. Sew one large black button to front side of loop through all layers. Repeat with second loop on opposite side.

not a creature
was stirring

...not even a moose

Kris Moose Wall Quilt
Pattern

Step 14. Sew small black buttons in place for eyes and medium button in place for nose.

Step 15. Apply walnut stain to slat and allow to dry. Base-coat cutout trees with dark green acrylic paint and stars with gold; dry. Dip sponge or stencil brush in medium green paint. Remove excess paint on paper towel. Tap edges and across center of each tree.

Step 16. With black fine-line permanent marker, draw stitches around edges of each star.

Step 17. Glue star to top of each tree. Glue a tree to each end of wooden slat. When glue is dry, apply a coat of satin varnish to front and back of hanger.

Step 18. Attach sawtooth hangers to backside of hanger. Slip loops over slat to hang. ✂

String of Lights Candle Mat

Continued from page 166

Step 7. Place backing right side down on work surface. Place batting on top and then appliquéd mat right side up. Pin or baste layers and trim backing and batting even with top.

Step 8. Center red jumbo rickrack over both seam lines between white ring and green plaid. Stitch through all layers with matching thread. When rickrack reaches starting point, trim about ½" longer than needed. Fold rickrack back on itself and stitch down.

Step 9. Bind outer edges with red bias binding to finish. ✂

Jolly St. Nick Stocking

Continued from page 152

Eye
Cut 2 white

Stocking Front
Cut 1 dark green

Sewing Guidelines

Basic Sewing Supplies

- Sewing machine
- Sharp scissors or shears
- Straight pins
- Hand-sewing needles
- Thimble (optional)
- Seam ripper
- Chalk marker or fade-out pen (for temporary marks)

An iron and ironing board, although not strictly sewing tools, are essential to great-looking projects. Don't be afraid to use them liberally!

Handmade Stitches

Buttonhole Stitch

(Sometimes called blanket stitch)

Working left to right, bring needle up at A, down at B and up at C with thread below needle. Stitches should be evenly spaced and of a consistent depth.

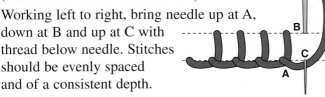

French Knot

Bring the needle up through the fabric. Point the needle at yourself, then wrap the thread or floss clockwise around the needle. Insert the needle back down through the fabric one thread away from the exit point.

Lazy-Daisy Stitch

Bring needle up through fabric at A, make a loop and hold it with your thumb. Insert the needle back down through fabric at A and up at B. Make a small anchor stitch to hold the loop in place.

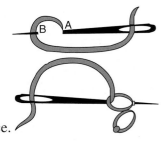

Slip Stitch

Slip stitches are worked by hand to make an almost invisible finish.

1. Work with a single thread along two folded edges.

2. Insert needle in one fold and slide a short distance.

3. Pick up a thread from the other folded edge and slip point of needle back in first fold.

4. Repeat (slide, pick up thread, insert back in first fold) along length of opening.

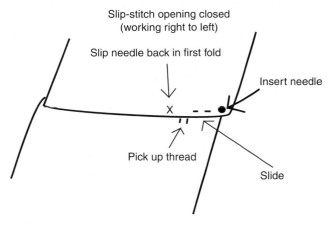

5. Bury knot between folds.

Straight Stitch

The basis of many hand-embroidery stitches, the straight stitch is formed by bringing the needle up at A and down at B.

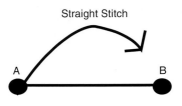

Satin Stitch

Satin stitches are simply straight stitches worked very closely together to fill in a solid shape. That shape is sometimes outlined for additional definition. *Note: Threads should lie closely side by side, but not overlapping.*

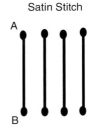

Enlarging Patterns

There are several ways to enlarge patterns—all of which are perfectly acceptable. Please choose the method that works best for you.

Photocopy

Photocopy the pattern provided at a copy shop at the percentage enlargement you want (100 percent is the size of the original; 150 percent is 1½ times the original; 200 percent is twice the size of the original, etc). If the shopkeeper objects, due to copyright infringement, tell him you have permission from the publisher to make one copy so you don't have to cut the book (show him this note, if necessary).

Grid Pattern

Any pattern can also be enlarged using a grid pattern. Draw a grid on the pattern every ½". Then, draw 1" grid on a piece of tracing paper or other lightweight paper. The final step is to transfer the lines in each grid from the pattern to the 1" grid. This is equal to photocopying the pattern at 200 percent.

Transferring Patterns

There are several methods for transferring pattern outlines and details. Choose the one that works best for your project.

Outline Pattern

1. Place tracing paper over pattern in book or magazine.

2. Trace with pencil; cut out with scissors.

3. Place pattern on the project. Pin in place, then cut or draw around the periphery.

Graphite Paper

When details need to be transferred as well as the pattern outline:

1. Place tracing paper over pattern in book or magazine.

2. Trace with pencil, but do not cut out.

3. Place pattern on the project; insert graphite or transfer paper between the project and pattern with the media side toward the fabric.

4. Retrace design lines with a dried-out ball point pen to transfer lines to fabric.

Iron-on Transfer Pencil

Another method for transferring pattern details:

1. Place tracing paper over pattern in book or magazine.

2. Trace with pencil, but do not cut out.

3. Turn paper over; trace detail lines with an iron-on transfer pencil.

4. Place pattern on the project with the media side toward the fabric.

5. Apply heat with an iron, following manufacturer's directions to transfer marks to fabric.

Satin Stitch by Machine

Machine-made satin stitches are often used to finish appliqué pieces and consist of closely worked zig-zag stitches.

Stitch Size

The width and length of the stitches are determined by the size of the appliqué and the body of the fabric.

1. Small appliqué pieces call for narrow zigzag stitches.

2. Large appliqué pieces call for wider zigzag stitches.

3. Fragile or brittle fabrics, such as metallics,

lamés, sheer organza, etc., require longer stitches to prevent damaging fibers and effectively "cutting" the appliqué piece out of the background.

4. Fuzzy fabrics, such as shaggy felt or synthetic fur, require wider stitches and a medium width.

Threads

Threads used for satin-stitch appliqué are chosen for their weight, color and finish.

1. For fine fabrics, those with small woven threads, choose a fine thread, such as silk, rayon, or thin cotton. Machine embroidery threads are a good choice.

2. For medium-weight fabrics, a medium-weight rayon or cotton thread works nicely. Threads in variegated colors add interest.

3. Heavy-weight fabrics might do well with a heavy-duty thread worked in a buttonhole stitch, rather than satin stitch.

4. Test threads of different weights and finishes on a sample of the fabrics in your project before making the final choice.

5. Select threads in coordinating or contrasting colors, as desired.

Helpful Tips

1. Thread upper machine with rayon thread and bobbin with a cotton or cotton-wrapped polyester thread in a color neutral to the backing, if the back will show. Or, chose a cotton or cotton-wrapped polyester thread in the same color used on the top if the backing will not be visible in the completed project.

2. Loosen the top tension slightly. This pulls the loop of the stitch to the back for a smooth look on the top.

3. When turning inside corners, stop with the needle down in the fabric on the inside (see Fig. 1).

4. When turning outside corners, stop with the needle down in the fabric on the outside (see Fig. 2).

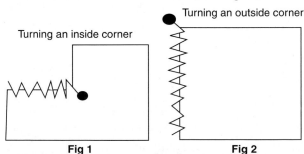

Turning an inside corner — **Fig 1**

Turning an outside corner — **Fig 2**

5. If the machine is skipping stitches:

- Clean the machine thoroughly, removing any buildup of fuzz beneath the feed dogs.

- Use a new needle.
- Try a needle of a different size.
- Match size and point of needle to the thread and fabric in the project.
- Apply a silicone needle lubricant to the needle, thread, and every place the thread touches the machine in the upper threading track.

6. An iron-on, tear-away stabilizer seems like an unnecessary purchase, but what it adds to the quality of a machine-appliquéd project cannot be denied. The product is ironed on the wrong side of the fabric under the area to be appliquéd. This keeps it from shifting during machine-stitching. When the work is done, the stabilizer is simply torn away. A touch of the iron adds the finishing touch for an appliqué project free of lumps and bumps!

Tea-Dyeing Fabric

Fabric can be dyed in a bath of strong tea to give it an aged effect.

1. Wet the fabric in clear water; squeeze excess moisture from fabric, but do not wring or twist.

2. Immerse in a hot bath of water and several tea bags. Allow to soak for 20–30 minutes.

3. Remove fabric; squeeze excess moisture out.

4. Hang fabric to dry, or dry in dryer.

Helpful Tips

- Fabric will dry lighter than it appears when wet.
- Conservationists warn that tannic acid in such a tea bath will cause damage to fabrics over a period of years, so this method should not be used on an heirloom project.
- 100-percent cotton muslin or broadcloth works best.

Gathering Stitches by Hand

Work a long running stitch close to the edge of the piece to be gathered with a doubled thread. Pull gently to gather. If fabric is heavy, use heavy-duty thread, such as carpet thread.

Gathering Stitches by Machine

To work gathering stitches by machine, set the sewing machine for the longest stitch possible (some newer machines have a built-in basting stitch). Pull the bobbin thread firmly and evenly to gather.

If the fabric is heavy, work a medium zigzag stitch over a strand of thin crochet thread. Then, pull the crochet thread to gather.

Topstitching Trims by Machine

Rickrack

To attach narrow rickrack by machine, run a straight stitch down the center of the trim. To attach wide rickrack, work a zigzag stitch or a broken zigzag along length of the trim.

Piping

To attach piping, baste close to the piping (use a zipper foot, if necessary) on one piece of the project with raw edges even. Place the other piece on the project, with right sides together, and stitch along the basting stitches through all layers of the project.

Cording

To attach cording or other narrow trims, work a zigzag stitch slightly wider than the trim with monofilament thread (for an invisible stitch) or with decorative threads for an embellished look.

Using Fusible Web

There is more than one kind of fusible web! The light or ultra-light versions have less adhesive on them and will accept machine stitches. The heavy-duty versions have a thicker layer of adhesive and are designed to be used without machine stitches. In fact, if you try to sew through the heavy-duty kind, the adhesive gums up the needle and causes a mess.

The best advice is to read the manufacturer's directions. Each manufacturer has a different formula for the adhesive and may require different handling.

Regardless of the type fusible product you choose, they may all be applied to fabric in generally the same way.

Fusible Appliqué

1. Trace the desired motif on paper side of the adhesive with a marking tool (pen, pencil, permanent marker, etc.).

2. Cut out around the marks, leaving a margin.

3. Bond the fusible web to the wrong side of desired fabric.

4. Cut through fabric, web and paper backing, following the drawn shape.

5. Remove paper backing and place the shape on desired background.

6. Fuse in place, following manufacturer's directions.

7. Finish edges with machine-worked stitches or fabric paint, if desired.

Special Thanks

We would like to thank the talented designers whose work is featured in this collection.

Mary Ayres
Nesting Hen Dish Towel, 35
Yo-Yo Tic-Tac-Toe Game, 84
Heart Pocket Scissors Keeper, 112
Autumn Leaves, 144
Embroidered Maple Leaf Pillow, 148
Christmas Tree Gift Bag, 162
Bluework Snowman, 164

Joanne S. Bembry
Floral Tissue Box Cover, 50

Nancy Billetdeaux
Kitchen Buddies, 37
Berry Special Baby Bib &
    Burp Pad, 72
Cool Citrus Table Set, 137

Kathy Brown
Blue Jeans & Bandannas Picnic
    Mat, 130

Holly Daniels
Chunky Colors Tote Set, 85
String of Lights Candle Mat, 166

Pattie Donham
Denim Duo Dorm Set, 82

June Fiechter
Big Bear Place Mat, 25
Aztec-Style Cosmetic Bag and
    Glasses Case, 56
Huggy Bears Backpack, 89

"I'm So Cool" Frog Pincushion, 120
Sweetheart Wreath, 140

Karin Getz
Pet Pals Place Mats, 12

Kathleen Hurley
Home Sweet Home Banner, 10
Jolly St. Nick Stocking, 152

Pearl Louise Krush
Patchwork Charm, 17
Pretty & Pink, 28
Classic Chic Bedroom Set, 47
Grandma's Posies Bath Set, 53
Cuddle Buddies Baby Car Seat
    Cover & Diaper Stacker, 76
Sewing Basket, 106
Thread Organizer, 107
Sunflower Bucket, 126
Woven Stripes Rug, 132

Janice Loewenthal
Bath Time Fun Hooded Towels, 66

Chris Malone
Quilt Block Posies Wreath, 14
Fuzzy Bunny Blanket, 60
Sew Happy Sampler, 109
Kris Moose, 168

Connie Matricardi
Watermelon Denim Apron Set, 32
Fresh as a Daisy Door Pillow, 88

Noah's Friends Play Pad &
    Finger Puppets, 92

Bev Shenefield
Wild West Place Mat & Napkin, 30
Sew Sweet Machine Cover, 114
Sew Sweet Armchair Organizer, 118

Marian Shenk
Floral Elegance Pillow & Candle
    Mat, 8
Ribbons & Roses Tote Bag, 52
Baby Tote, 69
Cowgirl Clothespin Corral, 133

Willow Ann Sirch
Folk Art Flag, 142

Charlyne Stewart
Poinsettia Wreath, 160

Diana Stunell-Dunsmore
Silly Critters, 98
Roly-Poly Lamb, 101
Christmas Cardinals, 154

Julie Weaver
Apple Orchard Kitchen Set, 22
Americana Starflower Pillowcase
    Set, 42
Americana Starflower Pillows, 44
Baby Animals Bib Set, 62
Baby Ducky Onesie, 65